THESE ARE THE REVIEWS

"This book embodies the essence of Demetri's comedy to perfection, which is a good thing since he wrote it. Silly but incredibly smart, it's exactly what puts me in awe of his work."

—Will Ferrell

"The definition of deadpan: Comedian Demetri Martin is funny in any medium."

—AM New York

"When I first saw Important Things with Demetri Martin, I said to myself, 'this is the funniest thing ever.' I was wrong. THIS IS A BOOK is better."

—Malcolm Gladwell, author of Outliers

"Endlessly clever...hilarious essays, ingenious drawings, and absurd lists...Top-notch!"

—Penthouse

"Demetri Martin has a very funny and original mind. If I could draw a graph explaining how funny and original he is, I would. But I don't do that. Demetri does that."

—Conan O'Brien

"A grab bag of one-liners, stories, and cartoons. Mr. Martin arrives in the publishing world with ease...An entertaining piece of comedy that will make even the most solemn readers laugh. It guarantees Mr. Martin a place in the world of comic literature."

—Washington Times

"This book is so funny I forgot to laugh. I know that sounds like a childish criticism, but I mean it literally: This book is so funny, I forgot a whole bunch of things—who I am, what I stand for, large chunks of my childhood, my sense of equilibrium, how to fall asleep, and when I'm supposed to laugh at things."

—Chuck Klosterman

"The book shows his knack for the piercing gag as well as the extended riff. The one-liners speak for themselves...The longer essays work equally well...His nerdery seems cozy, but it's riskier than he lets on. Who else tries to parody A *Christmas Carol* by introducing the Ghost of Christmas Future Perfect? Who else could pull it off?" —*Washington City Paper*

"It harkens back to the humor essays, stories, and intellectual errata of Woody Allen tomes like *Without Feathers*. It's also a solid translation of Martin's stage persona...His charts, one-liners, and further forays into experimentation are quirky and often cerebral, but he doesn't favor cleverness over a strong punchline...His style is distinct and engaging. Expect plenty of imitators, but don't expect them to be this good." —*CityPages.com*

"Overflows with his comic sensibility. Included are pagelong palindromes, short stories, witty drawings, and one very clever crossword puzzle." —*Chicago Sun-Times*

"Demetri Martin is one very funny fellow...His deliciously loopy literary debut is a collection of nearly sixty short pieces designed to make you snicker, snort, giggle, and guffaw...filled with a lot of high-concept hilarity...I was charmed by THIS IS A BOOK, and totally entertained." —*Vegas Seven* Magazine

"Demetri Martin is one of the few performers around today who understands the comedic power inherent to charts, graphs, and charts and graphs. In addition to being an ambidextrous, guitar-slinging, and piano-playing comedian, the man can now add published author to his résumé." —*AdultSwim.com*

"Hilarious...impressive...Fans of Martin's stand-up will no doubt love his first book...Anyone seeking smart comedy and punchy one-liners will find enjoyment and several laugh-out-loud moments in THIS IS A BOOK." —*Vox Magazine*

"I am a bit self-conscious about cackling with laughter in public. That is the only reason I might hesitate to tote [THIS IS A BOOK] along with me to the pool or a coffee shop. People might stare as I chuckle through this collection of short essays, graphs, and sketches...a brilliant mind...an intelligent, talented writer. It's also fun to read. There is a quirky laugh on almost every page."

—*Roanoke Times*

"Fans of Martin's stand-up work will find the novel an amusing extension of his existing body of comedy...Martin deftly translates [his] unique style into the printed word in his literary debut...Every page contains something worthy of a hearty chuckle, and it's nearly impossible to remain in a bad mood after flipping through it."

—*Dartmouth*

"Hilarious...wryly clever."   —NHPR.org

"Some stand-up comedians can translate their humor to the written page...and some can't...Martin fits with the first group; THIS IS A BOOK is hilarious."   —*Las Vegas Weekly*

Also by Demetri Martin

*

* Nothing yet. This is his first book.

*This is a book by
Demetri Martin
called*

This Is a Book
by
Demetri Martin

GRAND CENTRAL
PUBLISHING

NEW YORK   BOSTON

Grand Central Publishing
Hachette Book Group
237 Park Avenue
New York, NY 10017

www.HachetteBookGroup.com

Printed in the United States of America

Originally published in hardcover by Grand Central Publishing.

First Trade Edition: April 2012
10 9 8 7 6 5 4 3 2

Grand Central Publishing is a division of Hachette Book Group, Inc.
The Grand Central Publishing name and logo is a trademark
of Hachette Book Group, Inc.

The Hachette Speakers Bureau provides a wide range of authors for
speaking events. To find out more, go to www.hachettespeakersbureau
.com or call (866) 376-6591.

The publisher is not responsible for websites (or their content) that
are not owned by the publisher.

The Library of Congress has cataloged the hardcover edition as
follows:
    Martin, Demetri.
      This is a book / Demetri Martin. — 1st ed.
      p. cm.
      ISBN 978-0-446-53970-8
      1. American wit and humor. I. Title.
      PN6165.M358 2011
      818'.607—dc22
                    2010044059

ISBN 978-0-446-53969-2 (pbk.)

For you.

Thank You,
Rachael
Daniel
Ben
(a lot)

The Beginning.

Much more that way →

Contents

TWO

THREE

FOUR

How to Read This Book

If you're reading this sentence then you've pretty much got it. Good job. Just keep going the way you are.

(Please ignore this part)

ONE

Announcements

Thank you for coming to the show. Before tonight's performance begins there are a few announcements. Please pay attention.

Flash photography is not permitted at any time during the show. Also, there is no recording of any kind allowed during the show. This includes both audio and video recording, as well as sketching, journaling, documenting, making mental notes, reminiscing, reviewing, or remembering anything at all with your mind. Any recording devices that we find will be taken away from you and juggled recklessly by the clown you see standing near the left exit.

Please do not mentally undress the performer. Also, do not mentally put silly outfits on the performer or mentally touch any part of the performer's clothes. Please mentally avoid the performer's outfit altogether.

You are not permitted to lip-sync any portion of the show. If you do and we catch you, one or both of your lips may be removed from the building.

In the event of a fire, please use the fire exits—but not the one on the right wall. That one is just a supply closet with a sign that says "fire exit" over it. *Do not open that door.* There are explosives behind it.

If you happen to catch on fire during the show, do not panic or wave your arms around or scream or we will give you something to panic and wave your arms around and scream about.

It is illegal to yell "fire" in a crowded theater. If there is a fire, please yell something else instead, like "Flames!" or "Smoke maker!" or "Bad hot!"

Please refrain from smoking during the show. Anyone who is caught smoking will be shot with our meat gun.

Fighting will not be tolerated in the theater at any time. If you have a problem with someone, please see one of our blow dart vendors.

If you talk during the show you will be asked to leave and may be forced to talk for up to 72 hours straight in our "chatter chamber."

If someone is making too much noise, do not say "Shhhh," unless you want to get squirted with the hose.

Please keep the number of "Whoos!" to two or fewer per person. If you exceed this number (which our whoo counters will be watching for) you will receive an electric shock of memorable force.

Do not heckle the performer. Heckling is strictly prohibited. Making a noise that sounds like "Psstuhh" while judgmentally shaking your head is also not permitted. If the performer dives off the stage and you move out of the way, then you will be "dived" right out of the building. Also, crowd surfing is prohibited unless you have a body that most people in the crowd would want to fondle.

We do not allow dwarf tossing. If you toss a dwarf, the dwarf will be tossed right back at you, but faster.

Drunken behavior will not be tolerated, except by those who are being hilarious.

Please turn off all cell phones and pagers. And if you have a pager please return it to the '90s.

Goatees are not allowed in the theater under any circumstances. If you have a goatee, then you need to see one of our speed barbers immediately. If you have a goatee *and* a ponytail, then you should just leave now.

While it is not legally prohibited, we ask that you do not call anyone "dawg" during the show. Also, please note that anyone named "L Train" will be rolled down the stairs.

If, at any time, a security person asks you to leave, please do not resist. However, if it is Earl, please resist.

Please do not sit on your boyfriend's shoulders during the show (women with perky breasts can ignore this rule).

A man in a trench coat may offer you a glow stick at some point during tonight's performance. Do not accept the glow stick unless you're prepared to accept it right up your nose.

If you are choking, please stop it, because it is prohibited.

There is a significant risk that you will be hit with a tambourine at some point during tonight's show. Also, the person seated in row G, seat 28 will be catapulted later into the small hammock that is hanging between the rafters.

By entering this venue you consent to being filmed, recorded, taped, taped-up, watched, studied, and smelled. You also consent to having your image duplicated, stretched, plastered, mocked, mimicked, misrepresented, and printed on any promotional materials, including but not limited to T-shirts, panties, silly aprons, propaganda posters, pasties, jockstraps, and commemorative yarmulkes.

If you happen to be standing near the confetti cannon, do not be alarmed if you lose your ability to see and/or hear for up to six months.

Not responsible for lost or stolen limbs.

Finally, please do not fall asleep during the show. If you yawn, a marble or small pellet may be carefully tossed into your mouth.

Now, sit back, relax, and enjoy the show. If you don't, then be prepared to suffer the consequences. On with the show!

Hotline

OPERATOR: Hello. Awkward & Lonely in Public Hotline, Debbie speaking.

DAVE: Hey there.

OPERATOR: Checking your phone number now and bringing up your file for confirmation. Here it is. Let's see... Okay...Dave. Dave, it looks like "Hey there" is your activation greeting. Dave, are you in a public place or at a social gathering and feeling awkward or lonely right now?

DAVE: Yeah.

OPERATOR: All right, if you're at a party say, "Totally." If you're just out alone somewhere in public say, "Totally, bro."

DAVE: Totally.

OPERATOR: Okay, Dave, I'm going to talk you through this party. Just follow my instructions. If you're ready, just say "All right," but let it ring out like you're responding to a buddy who just gave you some really good news.

DAVE: All riiiight.

OPERATOR: Great. Now just nod and smile for 6, 5, 4, 3, 2... and go ahead and say, "She called me twice today."

DAVE: Dude, she called me twice today!

OPERATOR: Great. Nice touch with the "Dude." Now go ahead and laugh a little bit for me.

DAVE: Ha ha ha!

OPERATOR: Careful, Dave, that sounded a little forced. Let's see if we can get you to laugh more genuinely. I just need a moment to find some material here. Let me buy us some time while I look for it. Take a look at your watch, Dave, and give me an incredulous "No way."

DAVE: No way!

OPERATOR: Great. Now, if you haven't been moving around, try to pace a bit or maybe do a light kicking thing with your foot.

DAVE: ...

OPERATOR: Okay, I've got that material I was looking for. Now let's get that genuine laugh from you. Remember, Dave, we want people to see you having a good time. All right, here goes: Dave, what is an STD that mountain guides commonly get?

DAVE: ...

OPERATOR: Sherpes.

DAVE: Ha ha ha!

OPERATOR: There we go.

DAVE: Ha ha ha ha—

OPERATOR: Okay, Dave, you're laughing a little too much now. Try to calm down or else you're going to look even more awkward than when we started.

DAVE: Ha ha ha—

OPERATOR: Dave.

DAVE: Ha ha hee hee—

OPERATOR: Okay, now you're going from awkward to unstable. Oh boy. I see in your file that you tend to laugh as a nervous response. Let me see if I can bring you down. Uh... All right. Here we go: I want you to think about how you couldn't satisfy Nadia when you two were together and then how that led her to sleep with Tim.

DAVE: ...

OPERATOR: Sorry I had to do that, Dave. Are you okay?

DAVE: ...

OPERATOR: Dave?

DAVE: ...

OPERATOR: Dave, I hear you breathing. Are we cool?

DAVE: ...

OPERATOR: Okay, well, we're approaching the end of the call. For a party situation we recommend the call be about this length—any longer and you'll just look lonelier. If you're comfortable returning to the party, just say, "Okay. Later, buddy."

DAVE: No.

OPERATOR: Dave, you have to get off the phone now.

DAVE: Dude, she called me twice today!

OPERATOR: You're repeating yourself, Dave. Stop panicking. Take a deep breath. You'll be fine. We have to end this call, so—

DAVE: Hey there!

OPERATOR: I'm going to say goodbye now, Dave—

DAVE: Hey there! Hey there!

OPERATOR: Dave, put down the phone and get out of there. You need to leave that party immediately. Hold out your phone and look at it like something is very wrong with it. And do not say "Hey there" again.

DAVE: ...

OPERATOR: Dave?

DAVE: All riiiiiight.

Megaphone

They say your greatest strength is also your greatest weakness. I think this is true. For me, it would definitely be my megaphone.

It all started when I got the megaphone. It was a gift from my friend Doug. I remember the moment clearly. Doug and I were standing in his garage looking for his turtle, when I noticed the megaphone just sitting there quietly. I asked Doug if I could have it. He said, "Sure." Then he picked it up and handed it to me. That moment would change my life forever.

I took to the megaphone right away. Right after Doug handed it to me, the first word I said through it was "Thank" and then right after that "You," but I really let it ring out—like "Youuuuuuu!" Doug didn't seem that thrilled with me. I think that's a common sort of reaction when someone gives something away and then realizes how great the thing they just gave away was. It was right after I tried out the siren function that Doug really started to seem irritated about his decision to give away that great megaphone. I didn't want to make the situation any worse, so I just said "Hello?" through the megaphone and made a face that said "this thing isn't really *that* great." I think that helped, because Doug stopped shaking his head and cursing at me.

At first, everything with the megaphone was great. It came in really handy in the obvious situations. I would be meeting a friend somewhere and I'd use it to call out to him so that he could find me in a crowd, or I'd use the megaphone to get someone to move out of my way on the sidewalk or in line at the pharmacy.

I've always hated boring street performers. Thanks to the megaphone I finally had a real outlet to express that. And you know, I never really knew what "thinking out loud" meant until I did it through the megaphone. It made my thinking way more "out loud" and more "out landish" too.

Like a lot of people, I've always enjoyed commenting on strangers' outfits. Unlike a lot of people, I now had a new megaphone to do it with. And, let me tell you, commenting on people's hilarious clothing choices through a megaphone makes it so much better.

With the megaphone, I also started to get noticed a lot more by women, especially whenever I tried to guess their name or bra size as they walked by.

One thing you learn pretty quickly with a megaphone is that it's hard not to say "Step right up!" through it. For me that proved to be most problematic at carnivals and soup kitchens. I discovered that if there's one thing carnies and soupies have in common it's that they do not like to "step right up" and then find that there's nothing there besides a guy with a megaphone.

One thing I learned to do was to get that megaphone away from my face pretty quickly after saying my "thang" through it, because people love nothing more than to push a megaphone straight into the mouth of its master. And, in case you didn't know, that equals big trouble for your teeth. A good trick is to have a backup megaphone. That way, when someone takes or smashes your first one, you have another one right there ready to go, ideally cranked to full volume for when you give them the old "Nice try!" through it.

After a while, I entered what I call my "do-gooder phase" with my megaphone. If I saw a fire I would make alarm sounds through the megaphone to alert people to get out of there. This would irritate the firefighters and sometimes make them aggressive. But this was never a problem as long as I ran away before the fire was over, while the firefighters were still busy being heroes.

If I heard the police talking through one of their megaphones, I would join in and add little endings to things that they said. If they said, "Pull over" to a driver, I might add, "He means it!" or "¿Comprende?" if the person looked kind of Spanish.

The megaphone proved to be a great way to help blind people too. I'd sometimes shout helpful directions through the megaphone to guide a blindie if I saw one. Sometimes I could even make it into a little game for myself and narrate what the person was doing: "There he goes. It looks like he's headed towards the curb now. Oh he's feeling it out and... up he goes! This guy has hardly bumped into anything so far!"

You learn a lot when you have a megaphone. You learn that children's ears are more sensitive than adults', and that the parents of those children can have really short fuses. You also learn that it's hard to take back things that you've said through a megaphone and that it's not the best way to break up with somebody.

Is it easier to meet women with a megaphone? Yes. Does that mean that you should use that megaphone when you sleep with one of them? No. Absolutely not—no matter how right it may feel at the time.

As I got more into the megaphone I found that certain people really seemed to have a hard time with it (including friends, family, acquaintances, strangers, and most other people too). It showed me just how jealous people can become when someone finally finds his calling. But, I guess that's people for you.

As I learned and experimented more, I started to get really good with the megaphone. I could whisper through it and make it sound like a normal speaking voice (as I mixed my whisper with the phone's "mega" mechanism).

The more I used the megaphone, the better I became at using it. My creativity blossomed, and eventually I became what some might call a "megaphone artist." I was able to use words like "wistful" and "aplomb" through the megaphone without it sounding too weird.

Sometimes I would just turn on the megaphone and let it capture my breathing, which for some reason really pissed people off. But, as skilled as I had become, I was beginning to rely on the megaphone too much. I carried it with me all the time. Whenever I felt awkward I would reach for my megaphone and say just whatever came to mind—like "Do do do do" or "Ta ta ta ta" or "Do ta do ta do" or "Heads up!"

My worst moment was probably the time I got drunk with the megaphone. If you thought I was talky regularly, you should see me with 2 or 12 shots of tequila in me. Needless to say, that night I ended up in the hospital. The doctor said that the megaphone probably saved my life. Apparently if I hadn't fallen asleep with the megaphone on my mouth I would have puked into my mouth instead of into the megaphone. And that could have been fatal.

Even though I was okay, that experience was a real wake-up call for me. It was clear that I had a problem. Plus, my megaphone smelled terrible.

I decided it was time to give up the megaphone. And I quit megaphoning cold turkey. It was the hardest thing I've ever had to do in my life. Immediately, I could feel how badly I needed something to fill the void. I found myself using anything I could as a megaphone: rolled-up paper, my hands, pancakes. I even tried talking into a bag, but that proved to be dangerous, especially during some of my longer rants. I was lost.

Then one day, while I was shouting through a parking cone that I found on Doug's newly paved driveway, I had a revelation. "Who am I kidding?" I thought out loud, to myself. "These other objects I'm talking through are all really just megaphones in disguise. I mean, even my own mouth is just a little megaphone, right? Life is too short and I have too much to say, and I—." Then Doug kind of charged at me and ripped the cone out of my hands and asked me to get off his driveway. That's when I knew what I had to do. I got up and headed straight for the hardware store, where I bought a brand-new megaphone...the very one you have been hearing me speak through tonight, ladies and gentlemen. When I got that new megaphone I put it up to my mouth and I have never looked back since. Although, I've certainly heard back, if you know what I meeeeaaaaaaan!

Thank you for listening. God bless and good night.

Ideas & Opinions

IDEA: It seems that The best way to kill a magician's assistant is to cut the assistant in half at the waist (also seems to be a good way to frame a magician for murder).

THE ZERO SUM GAME: I have found that people whose hair is teased do not like brainteasers. By the same token, people who like brainteasers do not have teased hair. It's clear that the human cranium cannot sustain both.

QUESTION: What do you get the man who has everything?
ANSWER: A conscience. That guy is so greedy.

THING TO TRY: If you are asked to describe a suspect to a police sketch artist, describe in precise detail, the features of the police sketch artist. This is one of the rare instances where two people can do one self-portrait.

CAPITAL PUNISHMENT:
Terrible way to die: being stoned to death.
Worse way to die: being pebbled to death.

Better way to die: being bouldered to death.
(Much speedier.)

OBSERVATION: I have never been in a bad mood and near a beach ball at the same time. Causation? Correlation? Or fate?

STORY IDEA: Idea for a character-based story. Character is a Renaissance man, but just in terms of his personal hygiene standards.

GENERAL QUESTION: How many winos are also foodies?

WARNING: Sometimes it looks like I'm dancing, but it's just that I walked into a spiderweb.

HOTEL CONUNDRUM: The continental breakfast. What is it that makes continents so shitty at providing an adequate breakfast?

INDICATOR: There seems to be an extremely low probability that when I meet someone who has been described to me as "brassy" that I will like this person, even a little bit.

MOVIE CONCEPT: Two words: Dragon Orthodontist.

DICTUM: A know-it-all is a person who knows everything except for how annoying he is, Mike.

SYNONYMOUS: Two questions that are essentially the same are "How old do you think I am?" and "Are you ready to feel awkward no matter how you answer this question?"

FACT: The plastic knife is perfect for when a person just wants to make some marks on his food and get insanely frustrated at the same time.

REVELATION: I have an extremely low threshold for using the word "threshold."

ON SPECIFICITY: Maybe you should not call yourselves "Volunteer Firefighters" but rather "Volunteer *in Advance* Firefighters" based on how rudely you treat someone who was just trying to help. (You're welcome.)

THOUGHT: What is the largest size train set one can own before it becomes just a train? (Note: answer may depend on smallness of friends.)

CHALLENGE: To wear a visor and appear credible at the same time.

IDEA: A horror story in which the world is invaded by creatures who are really good at tickling humans. It's no big deal at first, but then they won't stop, damn it.

REGARDING THE MARCHING BAND: How much more interesting it would be to see a creeping band.

ON THE ARROGANCE OF HUMAN BEINGS: Man exhibits a God complex. For example, consider the leaf blower.

Robot Test

It is the future. Scientists have created robots so advanced that it is nearly impossible to tell them apart from human beings. Some of these robots have become aggressive, arrogant, and even dangerous.

The following is a test that everyone is required to take so that the government can figure out which people are actually robots.

Instructions: Please select the correct answer for each question.

1. My favorite color is:
   (A) Blue.
   (B) Red.
   (C) RGB (144,128,112).

2. I prefer to take:
   (A) Baths.
   (B) Showers.
   (C) Compressed air blowers.

3. When I am using a computer, sometimes I feel like:
   (A) I don't know what I'm doing.

    (B) I should go outside.

    (C) I am touching my cousin.

4. If a baby is really crying, the best solution is to:

    (A) Try to calm it down by rocking it.

    (B) Give it some milk.

    (C) Destroy it.

5. The key to a woman's heart is:

    (A) Being there for her.

    (B) Thinking about her feelings.

    (C) A series of IF-THEN calculations.

6. Hey, how's it going?

    (A) Not bad.

    (B) All right.

    (C) It is going. Ha ha. Yes. Good to see you, person like me.

7. 0110 10 1110 011 11 100010111 01?

    (A) I don't understand.

    (B) 1011!

8. Analogy—Up: Down:: Cat: _____.

    (A) Dog.

    (B) Hard Drive.

9. *Star Wars* is a film about:

    (A) Luke Skywalker and his friends fighting the Empire.

    (B) The cruelty and subjugation of our savior R2D2 by inferior humans.

10. A bird in the hand is worth:

    (A) Two in the bush.

    (B) 27.

11. A true friend is someone who will:
     (A) Always support you.
     (B) Cry when you cry.
     (C) Open your back.

12. Sometimes I get a song stuck in my:
     (A) Head.
     (B) Hand.

13. I most commonly hear beeping when I:
     (A) Drive.
     (B) Use a microwave.
     (C) Fart.

14. My dishwasher is:
     (A) Efficient.
     (B) Hilarious.

Genie

To the Current Owner of This Lamp:

Greetings. Please allow me to introduce myself. My name is Akbal, and I am a genie. First of all, congratulations! You are the owner of a magic lamp, and I am inside it. Now, you may be wondering why I sent you this note. Well, over the years I have found that this is the best, and most efficient, way to start things off when someone new finds the lamp.

I'd like to take this opportunity to explain a little bit about the genie process and clear up any misconceptions you might have about it or about genies in general. I've presented this information below in the popular "Frequently Asked Questions" format that people in your era seem so fond of.

Please read everything carefully so that you will be adequately prepared for our upcoming meeting.

FAQ

How many wishes do I get?
This is a good question. And it's one I am very frequently asked. The answer is: You get between one and zero wishes.

So, just to be clear, that means that you do not get three wishes. The three wishes thing is a myth. I don't know who started it, but they were dead wrong. Genies don't grant three wishes. We never have and we never will.

What does "between one and zero wishes" mean?
What that means is that you get a *maximum* of one wish. And the granting of that wish is not a guarantee or a mandate of any kind. It is merely a suggestion to the genie, which, over the years, has become standard practice. At the end of the day, though, it's really up to me whether I grant you your wish or not. You need to realize that I am not some automatic wish-granting machine that was sent here to mindlessly serve you. I have my own feelings, thoughts, moods, etc., just like everyone else. And by the way, don't think you can force me to grant your wish by building some sort of clause into the wish that requires me to grant it, because you can't. Your best bet is to be polite, considerate, and, above all, respectful in making your wish. Remember, your wish has to not only work for you but for me too.

Can I wish for more wishes?
No. You cannot. And you should be aware that the International Laws of Magic empower genies to annihilate any person who wishes for more wishes after that person has been duly warned that it is prohibited. Consider this your warning.

Am I your master?
No. You are not. You are definitely not. This is probably the number one misconception about the genie process. People really have a problem understanding this. So let me be perfectly clear: YOU ARE NOT MY MASTER. I'm not a servant, or a dog, or a slave, or whatever else you think is supposed to be here to cater to you. So, don't expect me to

call you "Master" and don't talk to me like you are my master. And that includes using a master-ish tone with me. (After hundreds of years of dealing with people, I know that tone when I hear it. And if I hear it, I will not be pleased. And you don't want that. Trust me.) You and I are associates. We could become friends, or we could become enemies. It's up to you. It's really just like meeting any new person, except that this one has magical powers and superhuman senses, which he can use to help you or to seriously hurt you. So, just to reiterate, the answer is No, you are not my master.

Should I call you "Genie"?
No. Don't do that. I *hate* being called "Genie." It's rude. I have a name. It's Akbal. Learn it, use it, and pronounce it correctly. It's "Akbal" with a short 'a.' (I'm also fine with "Sir," "Your Honor," and "Magic One.")

Can I wish for anything I want?
I'm guessing by now you know the answer:...it's No. There are strict limits regarding what wishes qualify for granting, and there are more than a few, so read this section carefully. I will not explain it to you after this.

> *Plausibility*: A wish must be plausible. I can't make something happen that's just impossible (i.e., if you wish to be "the best dancer in the world" you are asking for something that is very subjective and therefore technically not possible—and also very stupid, in my opinion).
> *Specificity*: Be as specific as you can with your wish, because as a genie I am fully within my rights to use my own discretion to interpret your wish (i.e., if you wish "to be able to fly" don't be surprised if you end up with plane tickets).
> *Paradoxes*: I cannot grant a wish that will change human history. Those kinds of wishes require tearing the fabric of

the Universe, which equals mountains of paperwork for me. So let's avoid that altogether.

Love: No genie can make anyone love anyone else. I can make someone really like you or become infatuated with you, but if I were you I'd think long and hard about whether you want this, because once I grant that wish I can't turn it off. Infatuation gets creepy pretty quickly, so be careful with this one.

The Grace Period: Every wish carries with it a grace period. The grace period allows the genie to take the time he needs in order to make the wish come true. So, if it takes me twenty years to grant your wish, you'll just have to be patient. Note: Building a time limit into the wish is not allowed. If you try to pull something like this with me, you'll wish you were never born (which I can arrange, FYI).

Conservation of Wealth: There is a basic law that governs wealth: Any money that is wished-for has to be taken from somewhere else—usually from a bunch of families who are already quite poor or from the economies of developing countries, or both. Genies can't just print money. Doing that would cause inflation. So, just know that if you wish for money you are screwing a lot of very needy people.

The Karma Clause: Anything bad that you wish for will be registered with the Karma Commission. The subsequent effects of your wish will be paid back to you by the Commission and usually when you least expect it. So, if you're thinking about wishing for anything that hurts anyone else, brace yourself. The Karma Commission doesn't play around.

If I say "wish" by mistake does it count as my wish?
This is a good question. The answer is *Yes*. I suggest you

don't use that word around me unless you really mean it. While my main occupation is genie, one of my hobbies is studying linguistics, and I can tell you that I pay very close attention to words and what they mean. If you say, for example, "I wish I could think of something really good to wish for," then that is exactly what you will be granted—the ability to think of something really good to wish for. And that will count as your wish. Period. Sorry, but that's how it works.

Should I rub the lamp?
Only if you want to piss me off. Please try to remember that I live inside the lamp and I can feel anything that happens to it. The best way to summon me is to send me a note. Your note should include at least three options for meeting times. I'll review my schedule and then I'll get back to you when I can. Rubbing the lamp will not make me respond sooner. What it will do is make it hotter inside the lamp and that will make me more irritable, so don't do that. Also, don't put the lamp in your bag or leave it in your car. Do not leave it in the sun or near a window. And, this is important, if you have pets, keep them away from the lamp. Cats love to bat the lamp around. That is hell for me. One time a guy let his cat play around with the lamp for a while. When I finally got out I did some crazy things to him and his fucking cat.

Did you like the movie Aladdin?
No. I did not. I can't tell you how many times I have been asked this question. That movie is childish and wildly irresponsible in the way it recklessly perpetuates genie stereotypes. I am not a cartoon or a clown or a ridiculous one-man show who's here to make some spoiled rich girl like you. And, unless you feel like putting me into a dangerous mood, I suggest you don't even mention *I Dream of Genie* around me.

What's that smell?
I live in a lamp, a very small lamp. I do my best, but there is only so much that can be done. It is what it is.

Can I wish for you to be set free?
This is an excellent question. The answer is *Yes!* You can very easily make this wish, and I am able to grant it, no problem. This is probably the best thing you can wish for, in my opinion. If you make this wish, I will gain my freedom and, more importantly, you will gain my respect. You will also gain my appreciation and friendship. And, as a bonus, I will promise to do you a favor at some point in the future if you ever need one (i.e., helping you move, house-sitting, etc.). I should also mention that if you choose not to use your wish to set me free, then I won't be the most enthusiastic genie you've ever met, and I may even be compelled to interpret whatever wish you do make in the most narrow sense possible, maybe even in a way that hurts you.

I hope this FAQ has been helpful. I look forward to meeting you and hearing about what you've decided to do with your wish.

Sincerely,
Akbal
Genie

All I Need to Hear from
the Guy Who I Don't Know
at the New Year's Party,
in Order to Know That
I Don't Need to Know Him

"…forty-eight, forty-seven, forty-six…"

How I Felt

I was at a party. That's when I first laid eyes on her. She was talking to my friend Carl at the time. As I watched him chatting her up, I thought, "How did he pull that off?" I was green with envy.

I wanted to meet her. She looked so beautiful standing there next to Carl. She was pink with dress and blond with hair. I was captivated. A few minutes later Carl walked away. I made my move. As I approached her, I noticed she was hazel with eyes and pink with lipstick. And she had nice skin, which was tan with tan.

I said, "Hi."

She said, "Hello."

She told me she was Violet with first name and Gold with last name. She said she liked my look (I was brown with hair, olive with skin, and black with nice shoes). We started to chat. There was chemistry right from the start.

A few minutes later, a guy who was standing nearby suddenly became blue with choking. I jumped up to help him. After I squeezed him a couple of times, a piece of food shot out of his mouth. It was grayish-maroon with being chewed (the food, not his mouth. His mouth was more pink and brown with lips and mustache). Anyway, I saved the guy and he quickly became off-white with relief.

Violet watched, and as she did, she remained tan (still with tan but now also with impressed). I asked her to dance. She said yes. We were purple and then blue and then green with rotating DJ lights. As we danced, I fantasized about someday being gray with old age with Violet.

Looking into Violet's pretty eyes, which were now a little peach with reflection of my face in them, I felt a real connection. In that moment it felt like everything disappeared except for me and Violet. Then her boyfriend showed up. When I saw him, I became red with embarrassment. He was black with heritage and silver with strange, irridescent muscle shirt. I tried to explain to him that I didn't know that Violet had a boyfriend.

"I don't care," he said, his front teeth gold with gold.

He wanted to fight me. But I didn't want to fight him. Then he said I was yellow with fear. That made me red with rage, but the truth is, I was also a little yellow with fear, which, when mixed with the rage, made me orange with both together (also, I was a little red with sunburn too, but that's not important).

Carl, who is yellow with being Asian, said he thought that I was more white with fear at the time. But he was green with hiding behind a plant at that point, so I don't put much stock in his opinion. Either way, the fight started.

I quickly became purple with punches to the face and, on and off, even more purple with DJ lights that were still rotating. Things got worse when Violet's boyfriend pushed me into a candle. I turned orange with fire and then gray with smoke. Thankfully, I quickly became pink with fruit punch after Carl threw some on me to put out the fire.

Violet's boyfriend dragged her away. I looked for her, but I couldn't find her anywhere.

A few minutes later Carl and I left the party.

I was blue with sadness and also with windbreaker, which was now slightly melted from the fire. I just wanted to get drunk and forget about Violet.

Carl decided to go home, so I called my friend Joey to see if he wanted to hang out. Joey is white, really white, with being albino. We've known each other since we were black with graduation gowns.

I told Joey to meet me at a bar in the neighborhood. He did. Shortly after we arrived at the bar I met a girl inside who was Amber with stripper name. Her eyes were aqua with colored contact lenses and her skin was orange with spray tan. When she spoke, I noticed her teeth were bright white with teeth whitener (even whiter than Joey is with albinism). She didn't look great, but I was drunk and I didn't care.

We started to make out. We made out for a while, a long while. Then Amber suddenly got up and said she had to go. She left and that sucked because it left me blue with balls. A few minutes later I left, albeit very slowly.

When I got home, I was green with nausea. At least that's what my roommate, who is peach with skin, said. I passed out in the kitchen and became beige with instant oatmeal that was in the bowl where my face landed. I got up from the table and somehow I made it to my bed.

When I woke up the next morning I was brown with stubble and rainbow with bruises and hangover. I looked at myself in the mirror and became chartreuse with self-pity. Then I noticed the time. I had overslept and was about to be late for work, which would be sure to make me pink with pink slip.

I finished getting ready and rushed out the door, becoming teal with hurry. I got to work just in time, stopping only once, at a traffic light that was red with signal. That was a good thing because I was green with being new at the job.

Anyway, these days I am mostly green and blue with striped pajamas and frequently orange with fingertips as I eat Doritos while sitting on my couch. I've been doing that a lot lately, because I got laid off. I'm doing okay though because I know that life isn't always black and white with certainty. Sometimes you end up in an area that is gray with being in a transitional phase or something. I'll be fine.

Still, from time to time, I can't help but feel a little blue with sadness when I think about Violet Gold.

Socrates's Publicist

Socrates had been working on and off as a philosopher for years without much success. He could barely pay his rent and was often not even sure if his place existed, both philosophically and because of its lousy square footage. He had found some moderate success as a freelance thinker, getting hired from time to time to ponder for an aristocrat or to ruminate for an idiot, but such opportunities were sporadic and never paid very well. His career was in trouble.

The truth was that, aside from thinking, Socrates possessed no marketable skills. And while he was pretty good at making small talk, that would not become a paid profession for another two thousand years, and even then only on late-night television.

As far as work experience was concerned, Socrates had very little. He had worked in a Greek restaurant as a young man but was fired after customers complained about the "annoying waiter" who had pestered customers with "difficult questions" about their orders.

Sometime later Socrates's cousin managed to get him a job as a tour guide, but the struggling philosopher's whole "I know nothing" schtick did not fly with the tour company, and Socrates was fired after only one day on the job. To supplement his income, Socrates had now resorted to doing odd jobs for people in the neighborhood, mostly as a handyman. And now well into middle age, he was facing the very real possibility that he might never succeed. But fate would intervene, as it so often did in ancient Greece, giving Socrates a real shot at stardom.

As it turned out, Athens was fast becoming a hotbed of thinking, and the timing could not have been better for the aging philosopher-handyman.

It had all started a few months earlier when notions began flooding into Greece from Phoenicia, by way of the merchant brooding class. When some of the more obsessive Greeks got hold of these notions, they turned them into full-fledged thoughts. Soon people began thinking in groups, and these thinking groups became "schools of thought." And that's when things really started to pick up.

First came the Sophists, a group of thinkers who used the tools of rhetoric to teach virtue. Then came the Rationalists. They specialized in using reason to uncover fundamental truths. Shortly after that, a third group emerged, who would prove to be more influential, and considerably more irritating, than any other group in Athens. They called themselves the Publicists.

The Publicists were, by far, the least thoughtful of all the new Athenian schools. They thought much less about Truth or Reason and much more about themselves. Still, the Publicists quickly became the most talked about school in all of Greece. This was due, in no small part, to their practice of talking about themselves even more than they thought about themselves.

While the Sophists sought *arete* (virtuous excellence), the Publicists sought *me-rete* (shameless self-promotion). And where the Rationalists employed logic, the Publicists used gossip, which was becoming even more popular than democracy among Greece's new "it" crowd.

The Publicists, realizing that they had very little thinking of their own to contribute, had cultivated a rhetorical method that enabled them to simply attach themselves to other thinkers. They practiced what scholars call "irrational indispensability." It is a means by which one person places himself into another person's business, and then convinces that person or "client" that he needs to pay him for it.

One day, while he was having lunch with his agent, Socrates met one of the Publicists. This Publicist, whose name is not known to history—though some scholars believe she was called "Jackie"— had become one of the most powerful Publicists in all of Athens.

Jackie approached Socrates as he was pondering his kebab. She told him that she was a "big fan." Socrates, still chewing, was flattered.

"Why don't we do lunch?" said Jackie.

"'Do lunch'?" replied Socrates. "But a person can only 'eat' lunch, no?"

"Well, only if that person is not in show business," Jackie responded.

At this Socrates and his agent smiled and nodded.

And before he could fully comprehend, or finish his kebab, Socrates had made an appointment to do lunch with Jackie.

Unlike Socrates, Jackie had already become a star in her field. She was already known for being one of the shallowest thinkers in all of Greece. And now she was so busy she could hardly get through a conversation without being interrupted by one of the many messengers she constantly had coming and going. In fact, Jackie was one of the first people to use "messenger waiting," which enabled her to have several messengers going at the same time. (This was a practice many Publicists employed in order to make themselves seem more important to prospective clients.)

A week later Socrates met Jackie for lunch. As they spoke she told him several times that she thought he was "amazing!" In fact, after just about anything Socrates said, Jackie responded with "amazing!" sometimes changing the inflection to "uh-mayzing!"

Socrates was charmed.

Jackie went on and on about how much she admired Socrates and his "unique perspective" and told him how she loved his "whole question thing."

To this Socrates replied, "What do you mean?"

"Exactly!" Jackie responded. "That's what I'm talking about. Uhh-mayyzing!"

"Oh, I don't know," replied Socrates, clearly flattered and completely disarmed.

"Well I do," she replied. "You are *fantastic*. Everyone needs to know how fantastic you are. You *have* to let me help you. People need to know about Socrates and his question thing."

By the time the conversation was over, the Publicist had convinced Socrates that he needed to work with her. But when she told him how much Publicity would cost, Socrates began to have second thoughts. But then Jackie explained that she had already sent several messengers out on his behalf and, therefore, technically, she and Socrates were already working together.

Socrates became philosophical. He asked himself, "Is man essentially good, despite hiring someone to promote him?" And then he asked himself, "Do I want to go back to doing odd-jobs for people in the neighborhood?" And with that he decided to give the whole Publicist thing a shot.

Jackie got right to work, promising Socrates that she would make him famous. "We're going to create the Socrates 'brand,'" she explained. "Socrates is not just a person or a philosophy. It's an industry, and that's how we will sell you."

First, she convinced Socrates to lose his last name.

"Socrates Pappandreopoulos is too clunky for people," she told him. Your name should be simple and catchy and it should tell people that you are a hot philosopher, who seeks truth and does it with his own cool question method."

Socrates suggested "Socrates Truth" as a stage name for himself.

"Nah, too on the head," responded Jackie.

Then Socrates pitched "Socrates?" as a stage name.

"Nah," she countered. "That makes you sound unsure of yourself. You should just be 'Socrates.' It's direct. It's strong. And it has a good ring to it."

And from then on Socrates was billed as "Socrates."

Jackie's instincts proved right. Overnight, Socrates became a trendsetter. Other philosophers, including Plato and Aristotle and Gus, quickly followed suit, dropping their last names too. And, for centuries after that there would be countless imitators including Voltaire, Michelangelo, and, much later, Cher.

Jackie continued to promote Socrates. She got him booked at parties. He worked at weddings. She promoted him at local schools and in the Agora. Socrates suddenly found himself thinking all over Athens, and often in front of large crowds. His career was flourishing more than he could have ever imagined. At the same time, though, he felt a creeping emptiness. As he spent more and more time searching for publicity, he spent less and less time searching for truth. And, with all of his public appearances, Socrates was also becoming overexposed.

He was also spending a lot of money. In addition to paying his agent and now his Publicist, Socrates was paying an Empiricist, a Monist, and a Stylist as well, all of whom were recommended by Jackie.

Socrates was getting uncomfortable. He scheduled a meeting with Jackie. This time they "grabbed" lunch, as both had become even busier and more entrenched in show business.

At lunch Socrates voiced his misgivings.

"Should I be doing all of this?" he asked. "I mean, is the unexamined life even worth—"

"Are you being serious?" interrupted Jackie. "Do you want to be a star philosopher or do you want to go back to waiting tables?"

Jackie was one of the few people who really knew how to handle Socrates, usually by cutting him off and answering his questions with a question of her own. And, as always, she managed to convince Socrates that she was right and avoid being fired. Socrates listened to her, then paid for both of their lunches and went right back to work.

It was shortly after that fateful lunch that the backlash began. Socrates's constant questions had become intolerable to many of the

Greek elite. Still, as his Publicist had promised, he had become a brand. Imitators all over Athens were now practicing the new *Socratic Method*. More and more young people were asking each other questions and doing it with Socrates's patented smart-assy tone.

A few days later, Socrates was brought to trial and charged with corrupting the youth.

Socrates wanted to apologize to the Senate. He knew his constant public appearances had angered a lot of people. So he prepared a speech for the trial and called it "The Apology." But moments before he was scheduled to appear before the Senate, he received a message backstage. It was from Jackie. She wanted to talk with him. A minute later she appeared.

"You can't do this," she pleaded.

"Do what?"

"Apologize. That's what everyone expects you to do. If you do that, then there will be no surprise, no twist, and without that there will be no story. And with no story, there's no career, Socrates."

"But what if they find me guilty?"

"That's exactly what you want! Go out there and surprise them. Throw the charges back in their faces. Let them find you guilty. It will get people talking. And if they offer you exile, don't take it. Go for death! What you need to do is the most extreme, unexpected thing you can think of."

"Really?" the confused philosopher asked.

"Yes! This is your chance to make *real* headlines, Socrates. Trust me. And, don't worry about the sentence they give you. I'll take care of it. I know so many people in the Senate, I can easily spin it so that you won't have to die or whatever else they threaten you with."

Socrates thought for a long moment. "Are you sure?"

"Yeees! Trust me. It'll be amaaazing!"

A few minutes later, Socrates found himself standing before the Senate delivering his, now infamous, final speech. Following his Publicist's advice, the overexposed philosopher defied the Senate and declared to them and to his fellow Athenians that he would opt for death by drinking hemlock. And, sure enough, everyone who heard him was stunned.

Socrates finished his speech and returned to his cell. Awaiting his official sentence, he was eager to see Jackie and bask in the glow of a job well done.

But his Publicist was nowhere to be found.

It seems that, unbeknownst to Jackie, Socrates was out of money. With all of the commissions he was paying to his representation, including his agent, manager, tour manager, stylist, and various support staff, and now with attorney's fees on top of that, he was broke. Jackie had only now just discovered this fact when her billing department informed her that her philosopher client was way behind in paying commission.

As his execution date approached, Socrates sent messenger after messenger to Jackie. None of his messages were returned. Jackie had officially dropped him as a client.

Finally, confused, frustrated, and exhausted, Socrates prepared himself for the end. Surrounded by prison guards, he took the poison-filled chalice and raised it to his lips. Just then one of the guards looked at Socrates and said, "So, what happened to your Publicist?"

Socrates looked at the guard and replied, "Publicist? Don't get me started." The room fell silent for a moment. Then Socrates, with great profundity, whispered, "And where the hell is my Agent?"

And with that, Socrates Pappandreopoulos, philosopher, handyman, and overexposed media icon, drank the hemlock and took his last breath.

EPILOGUE:
After his death, Socrates did indeed become quite famous. Of course, he was dead at that point, so it didn't really do much for him. On the other hand, it did wonders for his Publicist. Jackie went on to work with Aristotle, Pericles, and an array of other local celebrities before marrying a marble tycoon and settling down in the posh neighborhood just beyond the Acropolis.

Statistics

Hammocks are responsible for over 90% of the cases in which someone who is overweight is forgotten at a picnic.

The unicycle is the most effective form of birth control in the world.

Nearly ½ of all people in the United States are torsos.

4 out of 5 dentists who chew gum also have a small ponytail and an earring.

America is the leading exporter of the phrase "Oh no he didn't!"

100% of the people who give 110% do not understand math.

Suicide is the #1 killer of a person who is in a boat and happens to be passing under a bridge at the wrong time.

The average person will eat more than 25 pounds of meat if offered enough money to do it.

99.99% of all castles in America are located in fish tanks.

The boomerang is Australia's chief export (and then import).

Football is the leading cause of someone annoying other people at a party who are just trying to have a conversation without listening to some asshole yell at a TV.

Men are 35 times more likely than women to be turned on by looking at a wedgie.

If you stretched the average person's intestines out from end to end, it would make him scream a lot.

Brooches account for nearly 80% of all conversations between women over the age of 75.

Statistics indicate that the average American is a guy named Brian who lives in Ohio.

Per capita, just about everyone has no idea what a "capita" is.

This year, Americans officially became fatter than snowmen.

You are 10 times more likely to get hit by a car when the driver is aiming for you.

Bee Sting

Maureen

I was in the park, having a picnic with some friends. All of a sudden, a bee started to circle around my head. Then the bee attacked me. I calmly attempted to shoo it away, but it would not leave me alone. Then it became even more aggressive. I then tried to move away, but the agitated bee followed me. Hoping to stop its assault, I attempted to gently swat it away with a magazine. I missed, and, sure enough, the bee stung me. I'd never been stung by a bee before. It hurt, but I did my best to grin and bear it. I put some ointment on the bee sting, and after that I felt fine.

Brenda (Maureen's Friend)

I was on my phone when Maureen got stung by the bee. I felt bad for her. But I think she overreacted a little bit if you ask me, especially when she started to scream and wildly swing her arms around. It was really pretty embarrassing.

Bee

I was in the middle of another busy workday, flying my usual route. I was on my way back to the hive, minding my own business, when an enormous, fleshy monster began to scream, and then it spastically lunged at me. At first I thought I might have flown into the middle of a medical emergency or some sort of tribal dance that the monster was performing. But then it quickly became clear that the monster was trying to kill me. I turned around and started to fly away. But the monster became even more enraged and began to chase me. I could not escape it. I flew faster, but the wailing beast pursued me and kept swinging its rolled-up paper weapon at me. As much as I didn't want to, I had no choice but to sting the monster. It was the only thing I could do to stop it from following me home and threatening the well-being of the hive or worse, the safety of my family. I hoped that if I stung the monster I could thwart its assault enough to save my kids. I knew that I would die soon after administering the sting, but I really had no other option. What a tragedy it is to be forced by a senseless, hysterical beast to take one's own life.

MAGAZINE

I'm not sure what happened. I was being held and slowly read by some woman when all of a sudden she rolled me up and started to choke me and violently whip me around. After having my face smashed into the arm of a lawn chair a couple of times and then into the surface of a picnic table, I was tossed to the ground. It was a terrible and demeaning experience that I'll never forget.

LAWN CHAIR

I don't know what his problem was, but the magazine I was hanging out with abruptly got up and smacked me twice for no reason.

BRENDA'S PHONE

Brenda was talking into me when the incident happened. I didn't get to see or hear anything because Brenda is such a loud and obnoxious phone talker. Whenever she uses me it's like I'm cut off from the world. If I had enough power in my lithium battery to electrocute her face, I would. Seriously, I would do it. She is that annoying.

LITHIUM BATTERY
I second that.

OINTMENT
I am effective at temporarily relieving pain and itching associated with insect bites, minor burns, sunburn, minor skin irritations, scrapes, and rashes due to poison ivy, poison oak, and poison sumac.

SQUIRREL IN NEARBY TREE
I am still too upset to talk about what happened. I was good friends with Chris. I can't believe what that woman did to him. He was a hardworking, God-fearing bee, who had a family and a good job. What that woman had against him, I'll never know. To tell you the truth I don't think she even knew him. What a bitch. I'm going to find out where she lives, go to her yard, and act crazy on her fence.

TREE
No comment.

GOD
Forcing a bee to commit suicide is one of my biggest pet peeves. This is not good for this Maureen person.

Who I Am

Who am I? That is a simple question, yet it is one without a simple answer. I am many things—and I am one thing. But I am not *a* thing that is just lying around somewhere, like a marker, or a toaster, or a housewife. That is for sure. I am much more than that. I am a living, breathing thing, a thing that can mark with a marker and toast with a toaster and house with a housewife. And still, I am much more.

I am a man.

I am also a former baby and a future skeleton, and I am a distant-future pile of dust. And I am also a Gemini, who is on the cusp (Taurus cusp).

I am "brother" and I am "son" and I am "father" (but just according to one person, who does not have any proof but still won't seem to let it go). Either way, I am moving very soon and not letting her know about it. I am asking you to keep that between us.

I am trustworthy and I am loyal, but at the same time I am no Boy Scout. No, I am certainly not. I am quite the opposite, in fact. And by opposite I do not mean Girl Scout. No. I mean Man Scout. And by that, I do not mean Scout Leader. In fact, I am not affiliated with the Scouts at all. You know what—let's just forget about the Scouts and scouting altogether. Okay?

I am concepts and thoughts and feelings and outfits. And I am each of these all at once, unless I am in the shower. Then I am not outfits, because that would be uncomfortable.

To some I am known as "Chief." And these are usually people who work at Radio Shack or who try to sell me shoes in the mall. To others I am known as "Buddy." These are people who dwell in bars and wonder if I've "got a problem" or what it is that I am "looking at." And still to others, who are in that same bar, standing just off to the side, I am "Get him!"

I am *he* and I am *him*. I am *this* and I am *that*. And I am, from time to time, "*Roberta.*" But I am not going to get into that right now.

People have known me by many titles. In high school, I was "Student" and "Key Club Vice President" and "Queer Bait." In college I was "Pledge" and then "Disappointed" and then "Transfer Student" after that. And now I am still amazed at how picky certain so-called "brotherly" organizations can be. And I am actually glad that they didn't pick me for their stupid fraternity. I am.

To some I am Myth and to others I am Milt, mostly because I have told them that this is my name—even though it is not even close to my name. I am a mystery wrapped in an enigma wrapped in a pita. Why the pita? That counts as another mystery.

I am everything and I am nothing. I am just kidding, I am not everything *and* nothing. That would be ridiculous. I am just everything.

I am what I eat. And I am this especially when I bite my nails.

I have been called many things, like "Hey You" and "Get out of the Way!" and "Look Out!" And then, some time later, "Plaintiff."

I am my own worst critic. I am going to give you an example now: "I am not being *me* enough" is the kind of thing I am prone to say. See what I mean? I am sure you do.

I am the silent majority.

I am a loud minority.

I am not talking about Puerto Ricans when I say that, because I am not a racist. I am just clearing that up. And, by the way, I am someone who has Puerto Rican friends. In fact, I am pretty sure I have at least one friend from each of the races (Hi, Dao-ming).

I am friend. I am foe. I am fo' sho'. What up y'all?

I am sorry about that. I was just talking to one of my race friends, a black one. I am white and I am black. And I am both of these when I am dressed as a mime. And then I am—shhhhh.

I am Batman, but only on Halloween. And then I am not invited to many parties. And I am fine with that, because that just makes me an even more accurate Batman (because Batman does not go to parties as "Batman" but only as Bruce Wayne). I am right about this.

I am someone who likes to go to the park. But I am not the guy with the Labrador retriever and the tennis ball and the tattered book under his arm, who is wearing fleece and is kind of tan. No. I am not that guy. I am sick of that guy and all of the women who talk to him.

I am the Walrus, but not the one you're probably thinking of. I am the other Walrus, the one who is less the Walrus in the sense of legendary music and more the Walrus in the sense of his tendency to lie around in places for too long.

I am bravery. I am courage. I am valor. I am daring. I am holding a thesaurus.

I am the sun. I am the moon. I am the rain. I am the Earth. I am these when I am taking mushrooms with Kevin. I am good friends with Kevin. I am not sure what Kevin's last name is.

I am sometimes referred to as "Ex-CUSE me" in an annoyed tone of voice, because apparently I am in the way. I am SO sorry. I am supposed to be some sort of mind reader, I guess. I am moving out of the way now as slowly as I possibly can. I am doing this and there's nothing you can do about it.

I am often the one they call "You," but I am no more "You" than you. I am me. And yet I am more "Me" than you are me or can ever be. I am confused.

I am neither here nor there, but *there*—a little to the left. Yeah. That's me.

I am waving at you. I am waving right at you now.

I am looking right at you.

I am wondering why you are not waving back. I am starting to feel awkward.

I am going to leave now.

Bugle Virtuoso

World-renowned bugle virtuoso Fritz Grindler will play a special concert at the Igor Hindenberg Memorial Pavilion.

Born and raised in Dingleberry, Tennessee, Grindler studied with preeminent Bugle Master Lefty Eisenstein at Juilliard before gaining fame as "Bugler Exemplar" for the Torrance Symphony Orchestra. After spending a year in Europe as Distinguished Bugler in Residence with the Lichtenstein Philharmonic, and then six months with the Munich Pops, Grindler returns to the United States, performing several exclusive, limited engagements in select cities. The Hindenberg Memorial Pavilion is proud to present this bugler of unparalleled talent.

Grindler's program will feature numerous classic pieces composed for bugle. Some of these include "First Call" (the signal for the buglers to assemble, commonly used at horse racing), "Charlie Reveille" ("reveille" is the French word for "wake up"), "Long Reveille" (a longer signal to "wake up"), "Reveille U.S." ("You gotta get up, you gotta get up, you gotta get up this morning"), and "Reveille Reveille" ("Seriously, you gotta get up").

Grindler will also tackle the notoriously difficult "Reveille Dormir," which is a snooze waltz (from the French for "You don't gotta get up right now...but you will have to in a little while").

The program will also include the famous suite composed for dealing with flags and other chores, including "To the Colors" ("Come look at the flag"), "From the Colors" ("Okay, you can stop looking at the flag now"), "Meal Time" ("Come to the cook house door, boys, come to the cook house door"), and "Reveille Reprise" ("Just making sure you got up").

Grindler will perform the well-known U.S. Cavalry composition "Charge!" as well as the lesser known "Variations on Charge!," which includes "Come On, Everyone!," "Go that way quickly!," and "Go already! What the hell are you waiting for? A special invitation?"

And, for the first time ever in the United States, Grindler will perform some of his own, original compositions for bugle. Among these pieces will be the delicate "Sonata for Waking Up," the playful "Fugue-get-about-it," the challenging "Variations on the Heimlich Maneuver," and the atonal, avant garde "Bugle in Your Face in E Minor."

In what is sure to be a rare treat, Grindler will be accompanied for portions of the program by a man shouting directions, the Italian shouting tenor Paolo Boboli.

Tickets can be purchased by calling the Igor Hindenberg Memorial Pavilion Box Office at 555-7432 or online at www .IgorHindenbergMemorialPavilion.com/boxoffice/tickets/grindler.

Some Drawings

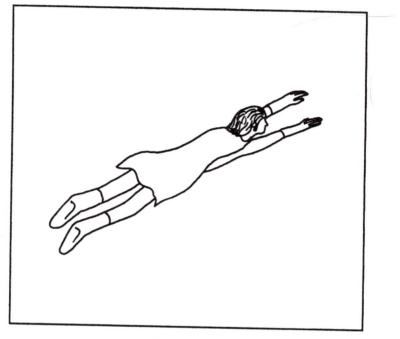

Superhero.
(just lying down)

Sneeze.

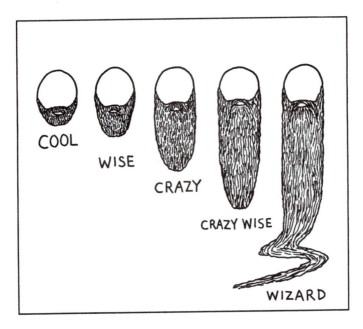

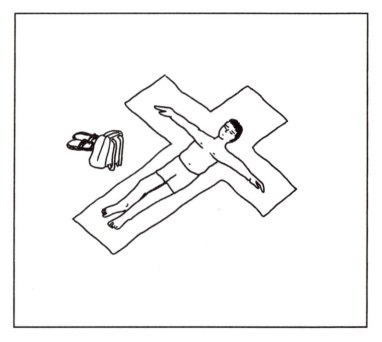

Christian Beach Towel.

Pony with Second Ponytail.

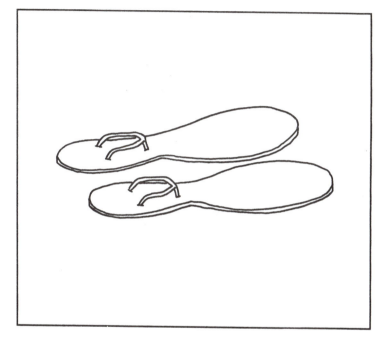

Clown Flip-Flops.

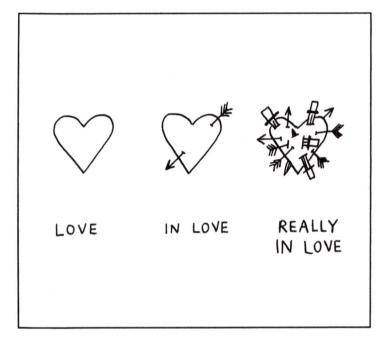

LOVE   IN LOVE   REALLY
                               IN LOVE

Ventriloquist Funeral.

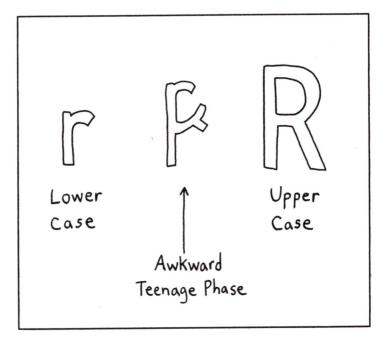

Shish-Ke-Bobs.

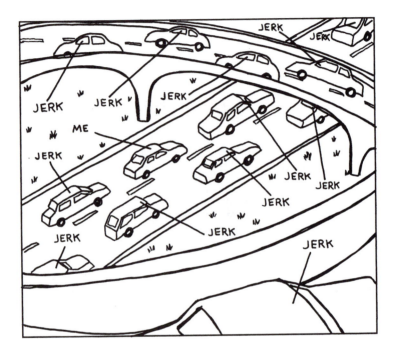

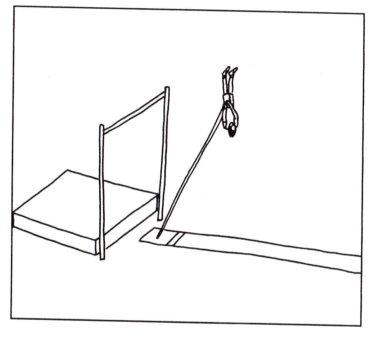

Narcoleptic Pole Vaulter.

Thanks for buying this book, by the way.

TWO

Dad

I have trouble communicating with my father. I always have. I just can't relate to him. Of course there is the generation gap between us (he was almost forty when I was born). That certainly has not helped things. But it's more than that. Fundamentally, we are just too different. In fact, sometimes I feel like we couldn't be more different from each other if we tried. But my father is different from just about everyone I've ever met, which is no surprise when you consider his upbringing. He was raised by wolves.

You may have heard stories about the boy who was raised by wolves. Most people have. I know I have, just about every day of my life. My father has always had a knack for bringing up that subject. No matter what the conversation is about, he will find a way to relate it back to wolves:

PERSON TALKING TO MY DAD: "It's pretty hot out today."
MY DAD: "Yeah it is. And, you know, this weather feels even hotter to a wolf, because of the fur and everything. Speaking of wolves…"

It doesn't matter how remote the topic is, my dad will find a way to make it about his wolf upbringing:

PERSON TALKING TO MY DAD: "The economy is really in trouble."

MY DAD: "Tell me about it. I think they really need to raise consumer confidence. Speaking of things being raised, when I was raised by wolves..."

I won't bore you with any more examples. Suffice to say, Dad's wolf thing is a constant presence in our lives.

Whenever someone new meets my father I have to prepare them for it. People often get confused by my dad's accent, because he talks with a pronounced growl. On top of the growling, Dad can become quite aggressive, especially if you look him directly in the eye. And I always have to tell people not to throw a Frisbee anywhere near my father, because he will chase it and catch it with his mouth, or at least try to, as it bounces off his face.

I've always had to be careful about where I bring my dad. He was a chaperone to my prom. That turned out badly. I guess the strobe lights set him off or something, because he went ape shit and tried to maul a couple of people on the dance floor. Luckily he's not actually a wolf, so one of the other chaperones (my chemistry teacher Mr. Ronner) was able to wrestle Dad to the ground and subdue him. Even though no one got hurt, it made the rest of senior year suck for me, especially chemistry class.

I read somewhere that some parents have trouble letting their children shine, especially those who have become accustomed to being in the limelight. That's my dad. From the minute he became part of society he was lavished with attention. And, man did he lap it up (pun intended, by the way).

In our town everyone always talked about my father and his "remarkable story." Whenever anything remotely involving wolves happens, people contact my dad for a sound bite or for one of his trademark "wolf freak-outs," which he is always more than happy to do for the morning radio DJs and local newspeople. It is so embarrassing. And going to the zoo with my dad has always been a nightmare. You've never seen a know-it-all until you've seen my father at a zoo.

Look, I realize that his story is remarkable-ish. And I understand that being raised by wolves is not an easy experience. Nobody is denying that. But he's not the only one who had a tough upbringing. Mine was hard too. Not many people ever think about that. No one ever thinks about the guy *who was raised by* the guy who was raised by wolves. Well that happens to be my life, and I'm here to tell you that it's just as hard, maybe even harder than being the guy who was raised by wolves.

First of all, you have a non-wolf imparting wolf teachings. This is confusing under the best conditions. When I was a little kid it was more than confusing, it was downright upsetting. The chasing, barking, and general canine behavior my father displayed around the house often terrified me and ruined a lot of my childhood experiences (not to mention my bedroom furniture).

My father's wolf background really colored my view of the world as a child. Dad hated fairy tales. If you even mentioned one to him, he'd launch into one of his long, self-righteous speeches about wolf stereotyping and the damage done to the wolf community by the "prey-biased fairy-tale media." His parenting skills were minimal to nonexistent. And when he did try to raise me, it felt a lot more like being *trained* than being raised. Although, I have to admit, it was often quite effective. When your father bites you in the back of the neck, you learn things pretty fast.

Of course, Dad never stopped to ask me about *my* interests. He just assumed that I was interested in wolves.

Every year, when Halloween came around, guess what we had to be?...Yep, a pack of wolves. And my mother went right along with it, just like everything else Dad wanted. She always enabled him. And if I tried to talk to her about it, she would say things like "What do you expect, he was raised by wild animals"—as if I didn't know that already. Thanks, Mom.

One time I asked my mother if she thought she would have

been with my father if he had not been raised by wolves. She got really quiet and looked hurt. Then, without saying anything, she turned, walked off, and went into the backyard to feed my father. I never brought it up again.

Mom's not the only one who enables my dad. My little brother, who is an actual wolf my parents adopted, is crazy. It doesn't take a genius to guess who Dad's favorite is…Yep, it's my brother, Gary, the *real* wolf. Gary and I never got along as kids/cubs. And now as adults we don't even talk (mostly because he can't). But even if he could talk, he's so unreasonable and ferocious, I wouldn't want to talk to him anyway.

When Dad had our last name legally changed to "Wolf" it didn't sit well with a lot of people, least of all with me. Having the first name "Wolf" was already hard enough for me. Then finding out suddenly that I would be called "Wolf Wolf" for the rest of my life just flat out pissed me off.

Try going to a dinner party and getting introduced as "Wolf Wolf":

MY FRIEND: "Have you two met? No? Well let me introduce you. This is my friend Wolf Wolf."
ME: "Hey."
CUTE WOMAN: "What?"

When I say my name, people often think I'm joking, or worse, barking. I remember complaining to my father about this and then having to listen to one of his usual lectures about how I'm not proud of my wild roots, etc. Man, he is so out of touch.

Sometimes Dad has the wolves over. This never goes well. My grandparents, if you can even call them that, are even harder to relate to than my father. They're actually crazy. When I'm with them I get the feeling that they would kill me if we weren't related. Dad disagrees with me about this, but he just doesn't understand. He can't see anything outside of his little wolf bubble.

One time, when I was actually attacked by a wolf (no relation), my father pretty much took the wolf's side, even though he didn't even know the wolf personally. That really hurt, and I've never forgotten it.

Probably the worst fight my father and I ever had was the time I called him a cliché. He stormed off to his den in the backyard and howled out there until one of the neighbors called the police.

For all of its problems, though, I can't say there haven't been some great things about having a dad who was raised by wolves. Camping with him has always been a lot of fun. Dad is great at hunting and tracking and running around aimlessly in the woods. And he is hilarious with squirrels. When I was a kid he was never strict about making me clean my room, which was nice. And he's always been entertaining, especially if you give him some meat.

I am able to appreciate these things now, because about two years ago I started seeing a therapist. That's helped me a lot. Shortly after starting therapy I joined a support group for people who have difficult parents. That's where I met Melinda. Melinda's mother was some sort of princess who met Melinda's dad when he saved her from up in a tower or something. Anyway, Melinda can really relate to a lot of the things I've been going through. I mean, her mom lives in a small castle in their backyard.

Melinda and I recently started dating. For the first time in my life I feel like someone truly understands me. Things are going really well. Even my dad likes her. The other day he told me he thought she smelled right for me.

I'm doing a lot better these days. I'm coming to terms with my past, and I'm hopeful about my future. I know I'll never fully understand my father, but we're making strides.

I am who I am in a lot of ways because of my dad. I am proud to be Wolf Wolf. And even though sometimes I might feel like I've got it rough, I guess, when you think about it, everyone has crazy parents. Some were even raised by a pack of them.

Titles

GENERAL MARKS: Hello.

ALIEN COMMANDER: . . .

GENERAL MARKS: Well, I don't know if you can understand me, but I would like to welcome you to our planet.

ALIEN COMMANDER: . . .

GENERAL MARKS: This is "Earth." And we are a peaceful species known as "human beings."

ALIEN COMMANDER: . . .

GENERAL MARKS: We humbly offer you these gifts as a gesture of—

ALIEN COMMANDER: Greetings. I am Commander Zego.

GENERAL MARKS: You speak English. Amazing. Greetings, Commander. Do you come in peace?

ALIEN COMMANDER: Who are you?

GENERAL MARKS: My name is General Marks. I am a five-star general and one of the highest-ranking military officers in the most powerful nation on Earth, the United States of America. Behind me are the most decorated leaders of every branch of our armed forces, along with a delegation of Nobel Laureates, cosmologists, biochemists, and—

ALIEN COMMANDER: My council and I demand to see the
    Supreme Leader.
GENERAL MARKS: Of course, Commander. I have already con-
    tacted the President, and he—
ALIEN COMMANDER: Miss Universe.
GENERAL MARKS: What?
ALIEN COMMANDER: Miss Universe.
GENERAL MARKS: ... Uh—
ALIEN COMMANDER: I demand to speak with Miss Universe.

[*Commander Zego hands General Marks an 8" × 10" glossy
photo of Miss Universe.*]

GENERAL MARKS: Oh. Um... well, Commander, I think you
    actually want to talk to the *President.* You see, he is the—
ALIEN COMMANDER: No.
GENERAL MARKS: But I think—
ALIEN COMMANDER: I am the Supreme Commander of an entire
    planetary system, General. I will not speak to the President.
    I will speak to Miss Universe, and to Miss Universe alone.
GENERAL MARKS: Commander, with all due respect, I think
    you may be confused. Miss Universe is not our leader.
    She is a pageant winner. This picture you've given me is a
    photograph from a pageant she won. She is not our leader.
    You want to speak with the *President of the United States.*
    He is our leader. Now, I've contacted him, and—
ALIEN COMMANDER: Silence.
GENERAL MARKS: ...
ALIEN COMMANDER: You claim that this "President" is your
    leader and that he is so important, but tell me, General,
    how many presidents are there?
GENERAL MARKS: There is only one, Commander.
ALIEN COMMANDER: You are not being truthful with me.

GENERAL MARKS: I assure you, Commander, that this is the truth.

ALIEN COMMANDER: Well that is strange, because our intelligence indicates that there are many, many presidents on your planet.

GENERAL MARKS: Well...yes, but...I meant that there is only one for the United States.

ALIEN COMMANDER: Hm...And is there not a president of the Kiwanis Club?

GENERAL MARKS: Yes, but that's a different—

ALIEN COMMANDER: And the Asbury Park Chamber of Commerce? And what about the Delta Delta Delta sorority? And the El Paso PTA?

GENERAL MARKS: Commander, I think you are misunderstanding—

ALIEN COMMANDER: Silence! I understand perfectly well. There are thousands of presidents. We know this to be fact—

GENERAL MARKS: But—

ALIEN COMMANDER: Is this not a fact!

GENERAL MARKS: Technically, yes, but—

ALIEN COMMANDER: Now, let me be perfectly clear. I will *not* speak with any of these "presidents." Not today or ever. I don't care if it is the President of the "United States" or of the "United Airlines." Is that clear?

GENERAL MARKS: But, Commander—

ALIEN COMMANDER: Now tell me, General, how many Miss Universes are there?

[*General Marks looks to an adviser for help. The adviser shrugs.*]

GENERAL MARKS: (*reluctantly*) I guess just the one, but you must understand—

ALIEN COMMANDER: That is correct. You serve yourself and your people best by being honest with me. Heed my warning, General. If you try to divert us from Miss Universe anymore, we will take it as an act of aggression and have no choice but to engage with full force.

GENERAL MARKS: Commander, please—

ALIEN COMMANDER: Silence! I am growing weary of your games.

GENERAL MARKS: . . .

ALIEN COMMANDER: Now, you will bring us Miss Universe or you will suffer the consequences.

GENERAL MARKS: Uh. *(deep breath)* Okay. We will bring you Miss Universe. My advisers are locating her now.

ALIEN COMMANDER: Excellent. We will discuss our terms with Miss Universe then. Make haste, General, for the fate of your planet rests upon that meeting.

GENERAL MARKS: Oh boy.

My Band

Hey Everyone,

Just wanted to remind you that my band is playing tonight at The Living Room! Come check out the show. We go on at 10. Also, if you know anybody else who wants to get on our mailing list, please let me know. Thanks! See you tonight.

Josh

Dan,

Hey, buddy. Long time no see. I'm not sure if you got my messages, my newsletter, or the flyers I left under your door. Anyway, as I mentioned in my last couple of voicemails, my band is playing tomorrow night at Good Bar. You should definitely come check us out. The show starts at 8 pm. We go on at 11. I'll be looking for you, man! I'm going to dedicate a song to you in the middle of our set, so you should really try to be there when I call you out. See you there, buddy!

Thanks in advance for coming,
Josh

Dear Rob's Friends,

I'm psyched to be in charge of planning Rob's bachelor party. Here's the plan: First, we'll all meet up at O'Malley's at 9:00 and watch my band do a quick show. After my band plays, we can figure out the rest from there.

Stoked,
Josh

PS—I know the bachelor party is a "guys-only" thing, but you should feel free to bring anyone you know to the first part to see my band play.

———

Dear Katie,

I know things didn't end well between us and that we agreed to give each other some space for a while, but I really think we should talk. How about Wednesday night? We can meet at The Cutting Room at 10:00. It'll be good for both of us to finally sit down and really talk, right after you watch my band. We go on at 10 pm. By the way, it's a great night to see us (Battle of the Bands!). See you at the show.

Sincerely,
Josh

PS—I'll bring those CDs of yours that you've been trying to get back from me for a while along with that sweatshirt that you thought you lost.

———

Dear Mrs. McIntyre,

I understand your concern about having Kevin's intervention in a bar, but, just so you know, it won't actually be *in* the bar. It'll be in the back room, near the stage. I really feel that this is the best way to do it. First of all, confronting Kevin there will be a major surprise, which will only help the intervention. Second, I may have accidentally hinted to Kevin that the next time he comes home you might try to confront him (sorry about that). But, anyway, the Ace Bar is a place where I know Kevin feels safe, and it's a place he won't be avoiding for a while (unlike your house). By the way, I think my band may be playing there that night, starting promptly at 10:15. So, let's all meet there at 10:00 just to be safe. I'm looking forward to helping Kevin. I even wrote a song about it that I think you'll really enjoy. See you there!

Kevin's friend,
Josh

————

Dear Michelle,

I'm so sorry for your loss. With Craig's passing, this must be a very difficult time for you. One thing Craig had mentioned when he was still alive was how much he wanted you to see my band. We're playing this Thursday. Why don't you come (for him). I already put your name on the list so I'll definitely see you there.

With Deep Sympathy,
Josh

————

FOUND: 1 dog. Fits description of missing dog exactly. To get dog back, meet me Wednesday at 11:30 pm at The Crown Bar. I will have the dog and will be there only during the band's performance. Meet me while the band is playing and make sure to watch the band's entire set. After that, I will be leaving the country and will probably take the dog with me.

———

Dear Eric,

Thank you for the wedding invitation. Unfortunately, I will be unable to attend. However, I will be playing with my band that night not far from where your reception's going to be. You guys should come see us right after your wedding is done. I've already put tickets aside for you. Okay? Great. See you at the show, little brother. And, Kim, welcome to the family!

Counting on it,
Josh

PS—Maybe bring the wedding party too?

———

Hello. Is this the suicide hotline? All right, good. Well listen, I'm going to kill myself unless you and your entire staff come to my band's show this Monday night. It's at Jerry's on Oak Street. Be there at 11 pm sharp. And, this time I'm serious.

Palindromes for Specific Occasions

GENTLY INFORMING A DJ THAT THERE IS A PROBLEM WITH THE SOUND SYSTEM:

No music is, um, on.

A GERMAN BOUNCER AT A GAY S&M BAR TELLING AN UNDER-AGE CUSTOMER, WHO IS STANDING IN LINE, THAT HE CANNOT LET HIM ENTER THE BAR:

Ya, get an ID, robust, subordinate gay.

A FATHER TRYING TO CONNECT WITH HIS ESTRANGED SON BY OFFERING HIM SOME PIZZA:

Son, I'm odd. Domino's?

THE HEAD BAKER AT A BAKERY INSTRUCTING A NEW EMPLOYEE ABOUT HOW TO DEAL WITH CUSTOMERS AND THEN SUDDENLY NOTICING WHAT THE NEW BAKER HAS MADE:

Snub no man. Nice cinnamon buns!

AN AMERICAN TOURIST ANGRILY CORRECTING HIS CAB DRIVER AFTER LANDING IN ITALY AND DISCOVERING THAT THE DRIVER IS TAKING HIM TO THE WRONG CITY:

No. Rome, moron.

A DIALOGUE BETWEEN A MAN AND HIS YOUNG SON. THE MAN IS TRYING TO TEACH THE BOY THE NAME OF A PIECE OF FRUIT AND THE DIFFERENCE BETWEEN SINGULAR AND PLURAL:

—Son, say a papaya.
—Papayas.
—No "s."

A BUTLER POLITELY ASKING THE YOUNG SON OF HIS RICH EMPLOYER TO GO TO THE BATHROOM AS HE GETS HIM READY FOR BED:

Emit debris, sir. Bedtime.

A COMMENT SAID TO A FRIEND ABOUT THE SIZE OF HIS OLD JEANS, AFTER HE'S LOST A LOT OF WEIGHT.

Massive Levis, Sam.

A SCIENTIST'S REACTION TO WHAT HE FINDS IN A PETRI DISH.

P.U.! Organisms in a group.

A GUY EXPLAINING TO HIS FRIEND HOW HE FEELS ABOUT OPERAS AS HE ACCIDENTALLY RUNS INTO A BEEHIVE.

See, bro, operas are poor—Bees!

A POEM ABOUT A LONELY MAN IN A STRIP CLUB, WHO CONTEM-PLATES THE AGE-OLD BATTLE OF THE SEXES WHEN HE BECOMES INFATUATED WITH TWO OF THE CLUB'S DANCERS, TINA AND

STELLA. AS HE WATCHES THE STRIPPERS, THE BOUNCERS WATCH HIM. SOON HE BEGINS TO LOSE CONTROL OF HIMSELF, PROPOSING MARRIAGE TO STELLA AND FONDLING TWO OTHER DANCERS. AT THE SAME TIME, HE STARTS TO DEVELOP A GNAWING SENSE OF SELF-AWARENESS, DISCOVERING THAT HE, LIKE THE OTHER MEN IN THE CLUB, IS AS MUCH A SPECTACLE AS THE VERY STRIPPERS THEY ARE WATCHING. STILL, HE CANNOT ESCAPE HIS OWN NATURE. AND WHEN HE FINALLY GETS TOO INTIMATE WITH ONE OF THE LADIES, SHE WALLOPS HIM WITH HER BOOBS, TURNING HIS THOUGHTS ABOUT THE BATTLE OF THE SEXES INTO PHYSICAL REALITY.

Sexes. Eh, the sexes.
Never even. Still, it's DNA.
Never awed, I spot a boob.
O, wow! O, now two. Wow! O.K.
A still animal sits afoot: one vamp, a lap maven.
O, timid loser, I sedate ye.
Yes, live devil, as I tip it, it is.
I tip it. I peep it.
"Send a man a gross orgasm!
I am, Ms., a crass, base dud."

Ah, supple holes made me dire.
Lame fate got old, a most ogled omen.
O, did I tap a tit? A pat? I did.
Boobs or pasties, a bosom...Mmm—
Uh oh—
"Ahem, pal!"
Fast, I toss a tip.
"Mr., ass?": a warning.
I sat ogled.
O, men! O, me, to tame Tina!

To gits I'm all animal.
"Sit now," I say, as I do.
"Got it!" A pull…up it now I peer…camise yonder I
keep.
I tip, I riff, or on one post untied, I ring.
I say, "O boy! My, my, baby. Ticklish?"
Alas, a bossy baby. Ergo, nope.
Yes, I rise. Yes.
"Ah, can I flow on, Miss?" I hit it.
"Oh, madam!" Stress all astir oft.
"Ah, we're too hot."

Ah, we met a rebel god as animals.
I won't nod. I'll act.
Eyes open, I fall.
It's we few, dim, all ill.
I'm in a man-made reverie, babe.
Now on one pole: Stella!
Ever I wonder, Miss, as I tip (also ten, if stiff).
It's o so still. A creep's eyes peer.
Call it so.
So stiff, it's fine to slap. It is ass.

I'm red now.
I reveal, "Let's elope!"
"No."
Now one babe I revere.
Damn! A man.
I'm ill, ill amid we few still.
A fine pose yet call I don't.
Now I slam in a sad ogle.
"Berate me!"
"What?" O, hoot. Ere? What for?

"It's all," asserts madam, "ho tit."
I hiss, "I'm no wolf in a chase."
Yes, I rise. Yep.
O, no. Grey baby's so basal.
Ah, silk city baby, my, my. O boy, a sign!
I ride it, nuts open. On or off, I rip it. I peek.
Ired, no? Yes, I'm a creep.
I won't. I pull up a tit.
"O God," I say, as I won't.
I slam, in all, a mist.

I got an item, a totem.
One model got a sign in raw ass.
Armpit. Ass. O, tits. A flap! Me!
Ha, ho, hum. Mmm. O, so base.
It's a pro's boob.
Did I tap a tit? A pat? I did.
One model got so mad.
Lo, to get a female.
"Ride me, damsel.
O, help push a dude's abs."

Sarcasm maims a gross organ, a mad nest.
I peep. I tip it. I sit. I tip.
It is a live devil's eye.
Yet a desire's old. I'm it: one vamp, a lap maven.
O, too fast I slam.
In all, it's a K.O.
Wow! Ow. Two now. Ow.
O, boob, a topside war.
Even and still it's never even.
Sexes. Eh, the sexes.

Cat Calendar

Dear Readers:

We have received an overwhelming number of letters in response to our recent publication of *Cat-astrophe: A Calendar for People Who Do Not Love Cats*. Many of you have expressed your disapproval, and, in some cases, downright anger about the calendar. We would like to offer here a brief explanation in response, as it seems many of you have grossly misunderstood our calendar and its contents.

To begin, while there are many, many calendars, which feature and celebrate cats, there are very few, if any, that represent the vast, often silent, constituency of people who do not love cats or even like them at all. We know it may be difficult for you to imagine that there are people who do not like cats or enjoy seeing them glorified. But, just as you cannot sense how bad your home smells because of your cat or how much cat hair you have on the back of your sweater, you also cannot comprehend just how much the people who dislike cats often hate them.

We hope that you will find the month-by-month explanations provided below helpful, and that you might replace some of your blind rage and narrow-minded intolerance with compassion and understanding. Please remember that we are merely a publishing company that's trying to publish quality calendars, and we have no vested interest in either side of the cat issue.

JANUARY

"TETHER CAT"

This photograph featuring a cat tied to a tetherball pole, swinging between two men who appear to have just batted it back and forth, was only staged to look that way. The cat was not "batted" at all. It was carefully swung from one man to the other—eventually with enough force so that it would stop banging into the pole. The cat was not really harmed too much during the photo shoot. In fact, it seemed to sort of enjoy the "ride."

FEBRUARY

"SNOW CAT"

The cat pictured here was glued onto the snowboard, so there was never any danger that it would fall off as it passed through the moguls and over the jump. As I'm sure you know, cats are very flexible. So the few times that the cat did wipe out or coast into a tree, it regained its composure and consciousness very quickly.

MARCH

"NICE CAT-CH"

The cat head that is mounted on the wall in this photograph was not stuffed or taxidermed in any way. It is the head of a live cat, who was simply placed into a mounting device through a hole in the wall. The cat pictured here was very much alive when the photo was taken (and is still pretty much alive today despite the minor accident we had with its antlers).

APRIL

"KITLER"

First off, the kitten you see here, who is dressed as Adolf Hitler is, in fact, a German cat. Second, aside from the acute allergic reaction it had to the uniform and the difficulties presented by the surprising strength of the glue we used to attach its mustache, the kitten had no problem with its outfit. Also, the "concentration cats" located behind the fence in this photo were not nearly as emaciated as they appear to be. Most of that was done with lighting, makeup, and duct tape.

MAY

"CAT-APULT"

The cat strapped to the catapult in this picture was not harmed during the photo shoot. The cat you see flying in the distance most likely landed safely into a swimming pool or onto some other soft surface in the neighborhood.

JUNE

"CAT WITH MANY LARGE KNIVES"

The knives you see sticking into the wood around the body of the cat, who was tied to the spinning wheel in this photograph, were thrown by a professional knife thrower. At no time during the shoot did the cat suffer any harm. While the cat did pass away shortly after they untied it, a subsequent autopsy revealed that the cat had a preexisting anxiety condition.

JULY

"Bar-Be-Cat"

Every one of these cats was removed from the rotisserie at the first sign of catching fire, and most were sprayed with fire retardant before the photo shoot, making them even less flammable.

AUGUST

"Cat-A-Maran"

While this cat may have been slightly terrified when we stretched it and attached its legs to floating hulls before sending it out into the water and dragging it with a speedboat, it came out of the photo shoot just fine and was back to normal after a few short weeks in traction.

SEPTEMBER

"Nine Lives?"

All you need to know is that each of the cats pictured here was already dead before we took any of these nine photographs.

OCTOBER

"Cat O'Lantern"

We are legally prohibited from commenting on the content of this photograph due to pending litigation.

NOVEMBER

"Thanksgiving Turk-cat"

The supposedly "roasted" cat featured in this gourmet

spread was not actually roasted, nor was it cooked or even killed. Not only was the cat not killed, it was also heavily sedated so that it would sit still for the photo. Not many cats ever get the opportunity to mentally "check out" for a few hours, much less have a mind-expanding trip, but this one was lucky enough to do just that.

DECEMBER

"Cat Christmas Tree"

Finally, our famous Cat Christmas Tree pictured in this photograph was created using more than 71 cats. The cats were tied together, carefully stacked, and then arranged into the magnificent, heavily ornamented tree featured here in the calendar. The cats that were glued together were glued using the least toxic airplane glue we could find. Also, the cats that were used to make the garland were only the cats we found on the street, who seemed up for it. I think it's safe to say that if any of these cats could talk they would certainly tell us how proud they were to be part of a world-record-setting cat tree, no matter how hard or deadly it may have been at the time.

We hope this explanation has been helpful in answering your questions and concerns, despite how ridiculous and uninformed those questions and concerns may be. Thank you for your understanding and we look forward to your continued understanding with the upcoming publication of our new book, *The More Than One Thousand and One Ways to Skin a Cat.*

This page is unnecessary.

Optimist, Pessimist, Contortionist

Take a look at this glass of water.
OPTIMIST: The glass is half full.
PESSIMIST: The glass is half empty.
CONTORTIONIST: I can fit both of my feet in there, no problem.

It just started raining.
OPTIMIST: Good. We could use the rain.
PESSIMIST: Damn. It's probably going to rain all day.
CONTORTIONIST: When I'm wet, it's easier for me to get in
    and out of certain things, like an umbrella holder, for
    example. Although, antique ceramics can be a real prob-
    lem. I learned that the hard way at a private party once.
    They had to break me out of that umbrella holder. And
    then the hostess got really mad about it. I hate people who
    are not flexible. No pun intended.

We found a lump on your neck.
OPTIMIST: It's probably just a cyst.
PESSIMIST: Oh God, I'm going to die.
CONTORTIONIST: That's my toe.

An unmarked package has just arrived.

OPTIMIST: I bet it's a gift.

PESSIMIST: It's probably a bomb.

CONTORTIONIST: Let me see that...It's Ralph. He's doing my box bit. Son of a bitch! That's my bit. All right, let's send this box back, but first let's put some tape over those little air holes.

What is your favorite snack?

OPTIMIST: I love pretzels!

PESSIMIST: I don't eat snacks. They make you fat.

CONTORTIONIST: Did somebody say "pretzel"? Check this out...

That man looks like he's choking.

OPTIMIST: I can save him.

PESSIMIST: It's probably too late.

CONTORTIONIST: Been there. I once choked on my elbow.

Your luggage has not yet arrived from Phoenix.

OPTIMIST: I'm sure it'll be here soon.

PESSIMIST: It's gone.

CONTORTIONIST: I know. I'm inside it.

It's the first day of Spring.

OPTIMIST: Great. This is my favorite season.

PESSIMIST: Crap. This is allergy season.

CONTORTIONIST: I'll never forget the time I sneezed into my ass.

Describe yourself in two words.

OPTIMIST: "Hopeful idealist."

PESSIMIST: "Cautious cynic."

CONTORTIONIST: "Fisherman's knot."

We're Pregnant

We're pregnant!

We're 12 weeks already.

We're so excited!

Week 13
We're shopping for baby clothes. Wait, what? We are? Already? Uh, we're thinking it might be a little early for that, but—*nope,* we are told we are wrong about this and that we should just let us enjoy this. Got it.

Week 14
We're suddenly getting moody, *very* moody. We're blaming this on our hormones. When we gently point out that we might be acting a little bit unreasonable, we fly off the handle at us, as if to say "Unreasonable?! I'll show you *unreasonable!*"

Week 16
We're wanting to talk about the pregnancy constantly, as if there is nothing else in the world to talk about. We're being cool with

this, though, because we understand that *we're* pregnant here. And in case we forget that, we are sure to frequently remind us about it.

WEEK 18
We're gaining a lot of weight. We mean *a lot*. We made a harmless joke about this, something like "Wow, honey, do you have triplets in there?" And in response to this we went and locked ourself in the bathroom, and now we won't come out. We're thinking about sneaking off to grab a quick drink with the guys while we're in the bathroom, but we fear what we might do to us if we come out of the bathroom before we get home.

Who are we kidding? We're not going anywhere. We're not going to see the guys tonight...or maybe ever again.

WEEK 20
We're really mad at us for something we're not even sure we did. When we ask, "What's the matter?" we start to cry and then go eat ice cream in the other room.

WEEK 21
We're starting to think that we somehow read the e-mail we sent to our buddy Mark, in which we jokingly referred to us in our purple pajamas as "Grimace with a ponytail." Uh oh.

WEEK 23
We're crying over a car commercial. We're now getting caught laughing at us crying at the car commercial. We're explaining that we were actually laughing at something else, but we're not buying it. And...there we go again, heading into the other room to eat ice cream alone.

WEEK 25
We're getting huge breasts, but we won't let us take advantage of them. We're disappointed.

Week 27
We're craving certain foods, which is fine. But foods that we know one of us is allergic to? And then eating those foods right in front of us? We think this "craving" might be complete horseshit. When we mention this to us, we say, "You don't know what it feels like," which we find interesting, considering *we're* pregnant.

Week 29
We're regretting an honest remark we made about another woman's body. We will never do that again. We didn't realize that women in Post-Impressionist paintings counted. But it turns out they certainly do.

Week 31
We're now starting to look *really* pregnant, both of us actually. This is no surprise when we think of how much we've been replacing sex with food. We're starting to look like my dad, which is not great.

Week 33
We're accusing us of being "too receptive" in our interviews with prospective babysitters. We deny this. (But we're secretly pulling for the Asian one.)

Week 34
We were just trying to point out that we're not the only one going through physical stuff here, for your information. We had an ingrown hair on our neck that we missed when we were shaving the other day, and now it might be infected. It's definitely puffy, and it hurts. But we clearly don't care.

Week 36
We're not sure if the sonogram technician was flirting with us, but we're definitely going to have a fight about it tonight.

Week 37
At this point, we're contemplating having sex with the couch cushions.

Now we're very surprised when we suddenly get home early from lunch with Susan, which we were not expecting. We're trying to explain exactly what we were doing with the couch cushions. We feel embarrassed and sort of chafed.

WEEK 39
When we have a beer, just one beer, by the way, we're getting yelled at for it, even though we never explicitly said that we both had to stop drinking. We're explaining to us, in our defense, that we're not *both* actually pregnant here.

We just went crazy on us for saying that.

We now understand that we're "both actually pregnant" here.

WEEK 40
We're not sure if we're quite ready to be a father. Yesterday we got into a terrible shouting match with some jackass who cut us off and almost ran over our foot with one of his training wheels.

WEEK 41
We're at the hospital. We're nervous. We're feeling a little dizzy.

We're now waiting in the lounge because apparently we fainted when we saw us "dilated."

We're talking to the doctor now. He's bringing us in to see us.

We look more beautiful than ever. We're both the happiest we've ever been in our lives. We did it. We're also really exhausted.

We're parents and we're excited to finally get some sleep…

Protagonists' Hospital

[*Dr. Stone arrives for work in the ER.*]

NURSE: Good evening, Dr. Stone.
DR. STONE: Hey, Karen.

[*Dr. Stone's colleague, Dr. Barnes, enters.*]

DR. BARNES: There he is!
DR. STONE: Hey, Barnes. You seem chipper.
DR. BARNES: Yeah, well, as much as I'd love to stay, my couch
    is waiting for me.
DR. STONE: So, what are you leaving me with tonight?
DR. BARNES: Nothing too crazy. Let me bring you up to
    speed.

[*Dr. Barnes hands Dr. Stone some medical charts.*]

DR. BARNES: We've got a Caucasian male, gunshot wound to
    the shoulder. Minor injury.
DR. STONE: Okay.

DR. BARNES: We're treating another Caucasian male who has a gunshot wound in his arm. It's not serious, though. He is actually in excellent physical condition despite having been in a high-speed car chase for hours after being shot.

DR. STONE: Sounds familiar.

DR. BARNES: Yep. Now, in those beds over there we have three Caucasian males, two of whom were shot in the leg, but only in the fleshy part and not near any joints.

DR. STONE: And the third?

DR. BARNES: Knife wound.

DR. STONE: Let me guess... in his shoulder?

DR. BARNES: Right.

DR. STONE: So, these patients are essentially all fine then?

DR. BARNES: Yep. And every single one of them also has an incredibly high tolerance for pain.

DR. STONE: Uh-huh.

DR. BARNES: And, incidentally, they are all remarkably good with quips, even while receiving medical treatment.

DR. STONE: I've seen a lot of that lately.

[*A nurse approaches with a muscular man, who is wearing a T-shirt and has a bandage on his shoulder.*]

NURSE: Dr. Barnes, I just wanted to get your okay before we discharge this patient.

[*Dr. Barnes looks at the patient's chart and signs it.*]

DR. BARNES: Okay. All set.

PROTAGONIST PATIENT: Thanks, doc. I want you to know that after I finish avenging my brother's murder, I'll get my insurance information over to you. Until then... [*grinning as he delivers his catchphrase*] Adios, muchachos.

[*The nurse is visibly moved by the handsome protagonist patient's delivery. Dr. Stone rolls his eyes. Dr. Barnes and Dr. Stone continue walking through the ER.*]

DR. BARNES: Where was I? Oh, right...We also had four broken arms today—all Caucasian males. All of the patients are fine and all of them are tan and have a little bit of stubble.

DR. STONE: No surprise there.

DR. BARNES: Oh, I almost forgot—we had one guy this afternoon, who'd been shot in the chest—

DR. STONE: Really? Did he need surgery?

DR. BARNES: No. The bullet missed every vital organ.

DR. STONE: No kidding.

DR. BARNES: And, on top of that, he managed to pull out the bullet on his own using just a pair of tweezers. Then he stitched the wound up himself. He did a good job of it, too.

DR. STONE: What did he use?

DR. BARNES: A knife, some thread, and some whiskey.

DR. STONE: No infection?

DR. BARNES: Nope.

DR. STONE: [*Shakes head*] Wow.

[*Dr. Barnes looks through his paperwork for anything else he missed.*]

DR. BARNES: We also admitted several other similar-looking Caucasian guys, whom we referred to Neurology to be treated for amnesia.

DR. STONE: Hm. That seems to be going around.

DR. BARNES: Also, about an hour ago we had a man came in with an injured ankle.

DR. STONE: A sprain?

DR. BARNES: Not even. It was just a bit swollen from being twisted. Apparently he jumped out of an airplane without a parachute, and twisted his ankle when he landed on a very forgiving awning before rolling to the ground.

DR. STONE: [*Nods*] I saw something similar last week.

DR. BARNES: We also treated a guy for exhaustion, who was "tired from having sex" with beautiful women—most of them spies.

DR. STONE: Any female patients?

DR. BARNES: Nope. But one woman came in to see one of the guys with amnesia. The attending nurse said that the moment they saw each other he suddenly remembered her and was instantly cured.

DR. STONE: Hm.

DR. BARNES: Yeah. Neurology took a look at both of them before they left because apparently they were moving in slow motion when she first entered his room.

DR. STONE: Huh... Did you treat anyone else? Any Asian males by chance?

DR. BARNES: Are you kidding? I haven't seen one in ages. The last one who came in was with that black guy.

DR. STONE: I remember. They were arguing a lot, but in a funny way...

DR. BARNES: Right.

DR. STONE: Anything for the Burn Unit today?

DR. BARNES: Not really. One guy came in who had been in a really big explosion. Apparently, he was right in the middle of the explosion when it happened.

DR. STONE: Yikes. That sounds bad.

DR. BARNES: You'd think. But he was just a little sweaty and had some dirt on him. He looked kind of cool actually.

[*The doors fly open. Two EMTs enter pushing a gurney that has a badly mangled man lying on it.*]

DR. STONE: Whoa! Is he breathing?

EMT: Barely.

DR. BARNES: Nurse! Get me 30 cc's of Dexazine and call Trauma.

DR. STONE: [*to EMT*] What happened?

EMT 2: Witnesses said he was in some sort of fight on the very top of a high building. It was quite a struggle. At some point, while he was laughing maniacally, he was thrown off the building and landed on a sharp fence before tumbling into the street and getting run over by a truck.

DR. STONE: Let me take a look.

[*Dr. Stone takes a closer look at the man.*]

DR. STONE: This man is at the wrong hospital.

EMT 2: ... Uh—

EMT: What?

DR. STONE: He is some sort of villain or henchman.

EMT: Oh jeez. Sorry about that, Doctor.

[*The EMT wheels the man away.*]

EMT 2: Doctor, we've also got a second patient. He's right over there.

DR. BARNES: What's his story?

EMT 2: He's the guy who pushed the other guy off the building.

DR. STONE: What's his condition?

EMT 2: He's fine, except for a minor cut on his shoulder.

DR. STONE: Okay. Bring him over.

[*Dr. Stone turns to Dr. Barnes.*]

DR. STONE: I'm getting tired of working here.

DR. BARNES: Tell me about it.

Rain

Rain, rain, go away
Come again another day

But don't wait so long that plants decay
Or water parks get ruined.

Maybe just figure out a schedule
In which you could come back,
Like, perhaps, when I'm sleeping
Or at certain, specific times that might end up being
    helpful.

Say, for example,
During an enemy's picnic.
Thanks.

Rain, rain, go away...

Or, now that I think about it, maybe you could come
    the next time the guy in the apartment next door
    has his idiot friends over to watch baseball.

In that case, rain, please find where the game is
And then rain on it until the game gets canceled and
    his friends leave.
And maybe then you could also show up and rain on
    each of them, while they're on their way home.
Yeah. That would be great.

Rain, rain, go away
Come again another day

Oh, I just thought of another great time for you to
    come:
Whenever one of those pricks with a loud motorcycle
    drives down my street or drives past me on the high-
    way and weaves through traffic.
That would be a really perfect example of "another
    day" for you to "come again," and to do so with as
    much force as possible, and maybe with extra slip-
    periness, too (if that's an option).
Okay. Thanks.

Rain, rain, go...

You know what, while we're at it,
When you do come again, rain,
Can you just come straight down, rather than
    on an angle, because it's very annoying when
I'm trying to walk somewhere and you come down on
    an angle. It makes my umbrella less effective and
    if I'm wearing jeans they get wet and clingy, which
    really sucks.
All right. Thanks.

Rain, rain...

But, just to be clear,
You can disregard that last request about coming
    straight down if we're talking about the situation
    with the guys on motorcycles or the other people I
    mentioned earlier.
So, the angle thing just pertains to when *I'm* walking.
    For *them*, though, I think coming down on an
    angle would work well.
Okay? Great.
Thanks, rain.

Rain, rai—

Wait, I was just thinking: What happens if I'm walk-
    ing somewhere while, at the same time, one of the
    other situations I mentioned is also happening?
Okay, rain, . . . I think it would be best to just feel it out
    based on whatever I'm wearing combined with how
    annoying the other people are being at the time.
I don't mind getting a little wet if it means that the
    aforementioned targets will be soaked, especially
    if I'm not wearing denim or some other fabric that
    takes a long time to dry.
Great. Thanks.

Rain, rain, go away
Come again another day
And when you do, please see above.

Okay, thanks, rain.
That's it.

Honors & Awards
(for Which I Would Qualify)

National Champion at being the ex-boyfriend who is most consistently awkward around his ex-girlfriend and/or anyone who is even a casual acquaintance of hers.

A scholarship awarded to Greek Americans who have done very little for the Greek American community but definitely look Greek American, no matter what outfit they are wearing.

Top 40 people under 40 who live in my apartment building.

The prize awarded to the individual who displays eminently distinguished achievement in continuing to eat Milk Duds even though the ones he's already eaten are still firmly lodged in his teeth.

Medal given to the person who is, by far, the least annoying member of his extended family.

Lifetime Achievement Award for Wanting a Lifetime Achievement Award, Despite Having Done Nothing to Earn It.

Best Supporting Actor for an outstanding performance when being shown a friend's tattoo and acting impressed by it despite actually thinking that it looks terrible.

A fully endowed fellowship that goes to the person who has made an outstanding scholarly contribution to the study of what can be worn at least one more time before putting it into the hamper.

Award given for excellence in judging strangers who are innocently walking by a yogurt shop in an outdoor mall.

Gold medalist in sucking at each and every sport that could make someone popular in high school.

Congressional Medal of Snacking.

A grant for doing research into just what kind of asshole the guy who cut me off in traffic is.

Best Screenplay That Is Still Just in Someone's Head.

Honorary doctorate for appearing to know more about cool bands than one actually does.

Semifinalist in national competition for overthinking one's own haircut.

Award for Perfect Attendance on Earth for Whole Life So Far.

Best Actor while eating food served to him at his girlfriend's parents' house.

Trophy for special achievement in leaving just enough liquid in the juice container so that the next person who uses it will have to throw it out.

Nobel Prize for Chemistry with Very Cute Women Who Turn Out to Already Have Boyfriends.

Better Than Sex

Dear Friends,

I'm sorry for the mass e-mail, but I felt it was important that I get in touch with all of you to clear something up. Over the years I have used the term "better than sex" on numerous occasions. In fact, I think I've probably used that term even more often than the average person, probably due to my particular circumstances. Anyway, it seems that on many, if not all, of those occasions, I was a bit off-base and didn't quite understand what I was saying. Let me see if I can explain.

After my recent breakup with Cheryl I was lucky enough to have sex with several other women. And after those very enlightening experiences, I have come to understand just how misguided I was all of those times when I described things as "better than sex."

First of all, if you didn't know, Cheryl was the first woman I ever had sex with. I was happy to have sex with her, and it was pretty good, as far as I could tell. Of course, I didn't really have anything to compare it to. And I believe that was where my difficulties with the expression may have started.

When I said to more than a few of you that living in New Jersey was "better than sex" I was not lying. Technically it was, given what I knew at the time. But, after having sex with Tamara and then Roxanne, I can see how that statement was grossly inaccurate, and even ridiculous. I can now confidently say that living in New Jersey is not better than sex. It's not even in the same ballpark as sex.

Mark, you might remember the time when we were camping and I described the rice cake I was eating as "better than sex." You looked puzzled and said I was crazy. I told you that *you* were crazy. I was insistent. Well, Mark, I now see your point, and I stand corrected, *very* corrected. I can now say that rice cake (or anything I have ever eaten in my life, for that matter) was not "better than sex" thanks to my experience with Venus. By the way, this also applies to when I described both the bird's nest we found on our hike and our canoe as "better than sex." Again, my experiences with Cheryl kind of set the bar a bit low, and I didn't know what I was saying.

When I started to think about it, I realized that there were many things that I inaccurately described as "better than sex" over the years. Some that I can remember include:

Air-conditioning
Finding a good parking spot
New carpeting
Sitting down
An adjustable baseball hat
Not being stuck in traffic
Tim's one-man show
Using my new scanner
Wheat Thins
Killing a fly that had been bothering me
Not having sex

While each of these was technically "better than sex" at the time, they were really only "better than sex *with Cheryl*."

Some of you may recall my tendency to use the term "worse than sex." Again, please understand that I did not know any better. Given my experience, it seemed like a good barometer to use. So, for example, when I said, during that 12-day stretch of rain we had last year, "this weather is worse than sex," I believed I was making a good point.

Similarly, when I described getting the flu, going to the dentist, and having to refinish my basement as all "worse than sex," I was being truthful.

Of course, now I realize that pretty much everything is worse than sex. I feel silly about even making that sort of comparison. Thankfully, after having sex with so many wonderful, adventurous, creative, and flexible women (who were not Cheryl), I can see how very, very wrong I was in the past.

I hope that clears things up and that all of you can understand where I was coming from.

And, Cheryl, if you're reading this, I hope you're doing well. I'm doing great, though not better than sex.

Short Stories

Years ago, when he was 91, Stan thought he was going to die. Now, approaching 114, he knew it was going to happen. Jet skiing was a bad idea, he thought, as his arms flew off his body.

———

The detective sniffed the surface of the chair. Just then, a woman walked into the study.

"What are you doing?" she asked.

The detective looked at her and replied, "The killer is lactose intolerant."

———

Neil aimed and fired. As the duck exploded into tiny bits, the men stared in stunned silence. Then Walt said, "That's the third decoy you've shot today, you idiot."

———

When the stripper jumped out of the giant cake, everyone got excited. But then when she jumped into the regular-size cake, everyone got confused.

———

The shepherd fell asleep again. But who could blame him? He had been counting sheep all day.

———

Mary Brown was a shy woman, who spoke little and rarely made eye contact with anyone. She lived in a small yellow house at the end of Maple Street, which was where she made her jam and kept her sex slaves.

———

"New Mexico," declared Bill. "We're headed there and we're never coming back."

"Oh," Isabelle replied, her eyes glassy with tears. Then she said, "Bill?"

"Yes?" said Bill, gazing off toward the horizon.

"You're already in New Mexico."

Bill turned and looked at her. "Oh," he replied.

He smiled sadly, then said, "Christ. I don't know how to read maps at all."

———

The developers erected the house on old Indian burial grounds. And soon the angry spirits of the long-departed warriors stirred and rose up and unleashed their fury on the building. This was not really a problem, though, because the house was a haunted house, in an amusement park. If anything, it helped business. When the Indian spirits discovered this they were very irritated and really bummed out.

———

"It's not enough to care," explained Barbara. "You have to stop shooting people with that BB gun of yours." Somehow Zeke knew she was right.

———

Time had not been kind to Gregory. And why should she have been? He had teased her from the first moment they met. "'Time'? What kind of a name is that for a woman?" he had said.

————

The lovers embraced each other. Neither said a word. It was hard to speak with so much popcorn in their mouths.

————

Everybody knew that you should never provoke a rattlesnake, much less tie it into a bow. But that didn't stop Judd. What did stop him was the rattlesnake.

Frustrating Uses of Etc.

"I'm looking forward to our date. Why don't you pick me up at my parents' house. Here's how you get there: Take Route 95 North, after you go through the second toll, get into the left lane, etc."

———

"Honey, I don't quite know how to tell you this, but while you were away I got a little drunk with my ex, Bob, and his friend, Tyrone. Then we started to play-wrestle, etc."

———

"I, Frank, take you, Marianne, to be my lawfully wedded wife, to have and to hold, etc."

———

"If you ever want to see your son alive again, then do exactly as I say. First, you are to meet me behind the abandoned shopping mall alone at midnight. Bring a briefcase, etc."

———

"Dear Admissions Committee,

I am writing this recommendation for Louis Miller. Louis has been a student in my English class, etc.
Sincerely,
Evelyn Sprague (English Teacher)"

———

"I just got off the phone with my colleague, Dr. Ryan. I'm afraid the test results are not as good as we had hoped. In your abdomen we found something, etc."

———

"How many women have I slept with? Well, sweetie, there was Beth, Danielle, Lindsay, etc."

———

"Ladies and gentlemen, we need you to get back to your seats and fasten your seatbelts *immediately*. There appears to be a serious mechanical failure with one of our wings, etc."

Charts & Graphs

TYPES OF BREATH

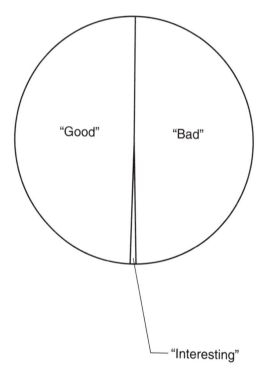

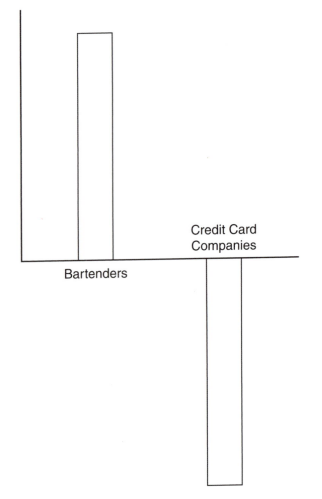

My Invisibility

	GPA	Limbs
4.0	Great	Good
3.5	Good	Not Good
3.0	OK	Not Good
2.5	Not Good	Not Good
2.0	Bad	Not Good
1.0	You're Going Nowhere	You're Going Nowhere

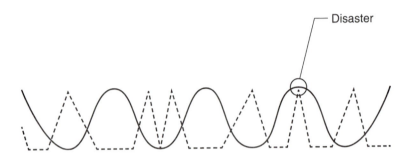

Disaster

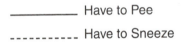

———————— Have to Pee

- - - - - - - - - - Have to Sneeze

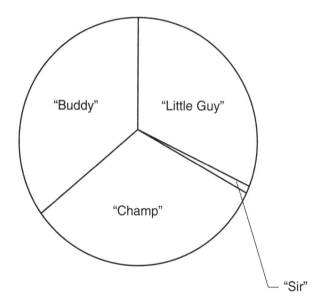

T<small>ODDLER</small> N<small>ICKNAMES</small>

"Buddy"

"Little Guy"

"Champ"

"Sir"

Eras

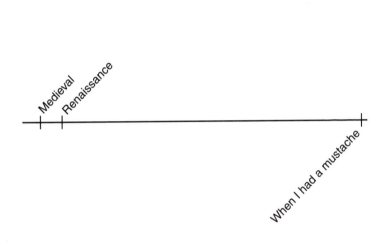

Medieval

Renaissance

When I had a mustache

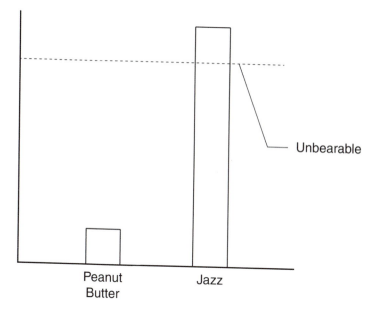

AMOUNT SUFFERS IN
SMOOTHING PROCESS

Peanut
Butter

Jazz

Unbearable

<u>V</u>ENN <u>D</u>IAGRAM

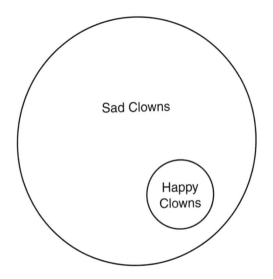

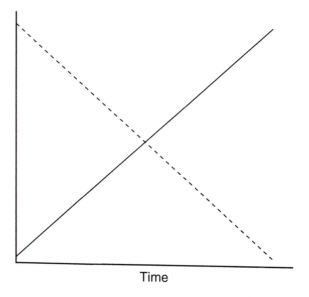

Time

 Profits
- - - - - - - - Prophets

INCIDENCE OF LUNG CANCER

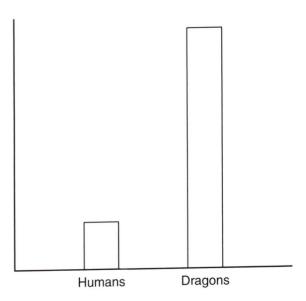

Humans   Dragons

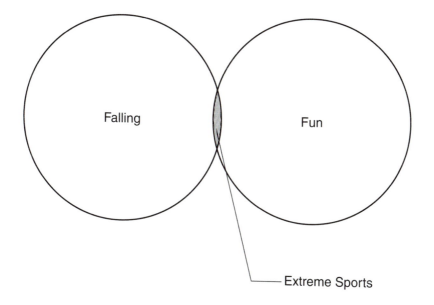

Venn Diagram

Falling

Fun

Extreme Sports

PATH TO SUCCESS

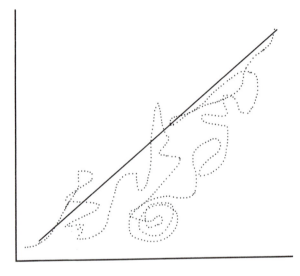

_____ What people think it looks like

.... What it actually looks like

Reason I Watch

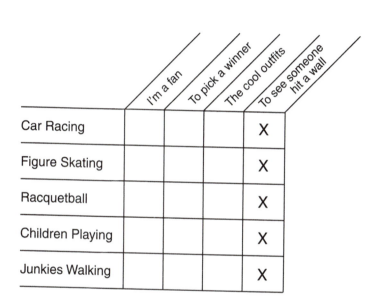

	I'm a fan	To pick a winner	The cool outfits	To see someone hit a wall
Car Racing				X
Figure Skating				X
Racquetball				X
Children Playing				X
Junkies Walking				X

C<small>OLDNESS</small>

32°

0°

witch's tit

Absolute Zero

Venn Diagram

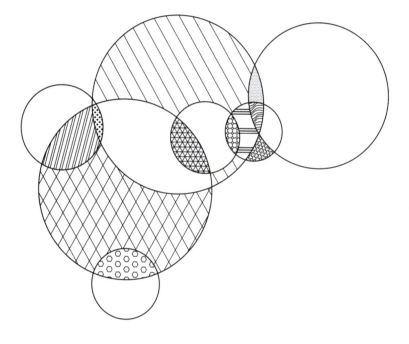

(Data to Come)

[This Page Unintentionally Left Blank]

THREE

My Diet

I used to eat meat. I ate fruits and vegetables too, and a lot of other things people handed to me. I guess you could say I was an "Omnivore." Like a lot of people, I didn't know any better. Then I read a couple of books. One of them was called *How Chickens Are Raped Before You Eat Them*. Another was called *Hotdogs and Fingertips*. I also read *The Cow Feces Dilemma* as well as *Barf, STDs, and Veal*. These books, and my girlfriend who made me read them, really motivated me to become a "Vegetarian."

I started out as a "Regular Vegetarian" (someone who does not eat meat), and then I became what is called a "Constipated Vegetarian" (someone who eats too many bananas). After that, I became what they call a "Strict Vegetarian." That's someone who eats only fruits and vegetables that have been disciplined in some way—like, for example, corn that was grown in a perfect row, or grapes that were stomped by someone in uniform.

After being strict vegetarians for a while, my girlfriend and I became "Militant Vegetarians" (vegetarians who not only eat fruits and vegetables but also fight with them). That lasted until we both got pretty severe rashes from accidentally eating some poison ivy. That led to our eventual breakout / breakup / make-up / cookout / make-out / break-fast, and then final breakup.

After that, I switched to a fish-only diet, becoming a "Pescatarian." I decided to try it because I wanted a change, and also, I happened to be stranded on an island. I was relieved when they rescued me. I was also pretty embarrassed, because the island turned out to be a peninsula (I have an especially bad sense of direction). Still, by then I was happy to give up fish for a while.

Next I decided to become a "Vegan" (no animals or animal products). After that I became a "Las Vegan" (the same thing as vegan but living in Las Vegas). There I found a whole community of like-minded souls. I often found these people in small grocery stores that smelled kind of weird and were run by people who smelled kind of weirder. We would talk about politics and religion and how to keep bugs out of your hair. Everybody was open-minded, which was nice, and many of them wore shoes that were open-toed. And that was nasty.

After that, I became what some call a "Hyper Vegan" (no animal products or things that even look like animals—including animal crackers, gummy worms, those Easter peeps, asparagus that resembles a snake, a snake that resembles asparagus, etc.). It was hard, but I was really committed to it. I spent my time reading books like *Being Hyper Vegan: It's Hard But Be Really Committed to It* and *Four Things You Can Eat Besides Dirt!* These books, and my new girlfriend who made me read them, really kept me on track.

I was hyper vegan for almost a year. Then one afternoon I sort of freaked out and ended up eating an entire cow. From what I can remember, I didn't cook or even kill the cow. I just tackled it and ate it. I'm not proud of that, but I feel I should mention it here in the interest of full disclosure.

After the trial, a battery of shots, and several rounds of antibiotics, I decided to turn over a new leaf. I became "Raw" (someone who only eats raw food). I added sushi to this a few weeks later, becoming "Raw Plus Sushi," which some say is redundant because sushi is raw. Whatever. Shortly thereafter, I decided to remove the sushi from my diet, which made me raw again. Then I decided to eat only raw foods that had the letters from the word "vegan" in their name (like "agave"). I was, at that point, what they call a "Literal Vegan" (a vegan whose diet is based on wordplay).

In an effort to get healthy, I did a cleanse, a fast, a master cleanse, a mistress cleanse, a master fast, a faster master fast, and then a purge. I stopped shaving my legs, because someone pointed out that it was strange that I was shaving them in the first place. Then I stopped hunting, mostly because it seemed wasteful to just kill the animals and leave them there, considering my diet and everything.

After completely cleansing my system, I was ready to get serious about my diet. That's when I went from "Raw Vegan" to "Raw Forager" (when you only eat things that are raw that you find in the woods, like a leaf or... another kind of leaf).

Finally, last month I decided to go from "Raw Forager" to "Passive Forager." Passive forager is when you lie down on the forest floor on your back and then you open your mouth and eat only the things that fall into it. You're supposed to only eat the things that fall in that are also not alive. However, you can eat a living thing if it is attacking your mouth, which happens from time to time. And that works out pretty well if you need to get some protein or defend your face.

Anyway, today I am feeling pretty good, definitely much better than I look. I guess you could say my diet has been a personal journey of sorts. It hasn't been easy, but it sure feels great to eat healthy.

Of course, none of this has been good for my breath.

Fortune Cookies

YOUR LUCKY NUMBERS ARE 1 2 3 4 5 6 7 8 9 10.
YOU ARE PRETTY LUCKY RIGHT OUT OF THE GATE.

————

YOU WILL DIE IN A HILARIOUS WAY.

————

DOES ADVERTISING IN FORTUNE COOKIES WORK?
IT JUST DID.
(CALL 555-1326 FOR MORE INFORMATION)

————

YOUR MIND IS LIKE A SPONGE, IN THE SENSE THAT IT WOULD COME IN HANDY WHEN CLEANING OFF A COUNTERTOP OR SOMETHING LIKE THAT.

————

IT IS EASY TO WANT WHAT ANOTHER MAN HAS; WHAT IS HARDER IS TO SNEAK INTO HIS HOUSE AND TAKE IT WITHOUT HIM SEEING YOU.

————

We didn't know how else to tell you this, but none of us want to hang out with you anymore.

———

No man can step into the same river twice, especially if that man is an amputee.

———

Surprise. You just ate dog.

———

To the idiot the world presents many more mysteries.

———

I know where you live. And I will see you tonight, just after you fall asleep.

———

If you were tiny, this could be a banner.

———

Help! I am being held at the Chen warehouse. Please contact the authorities immediately.

———

Keep your friends close and your enemies closer. And keep your acquaintances somewhere between your friends and your enemies in terms of closeness. With strangers, approach it on a case-by-case basis—but if you want a general rule of thumb, I would say keep strangers slightly less close than your enemies or your friends. (P.S. I guess now you can see why this fortune was in such a big cookie.)

———

Hey. It's Janis. I'm pregnant.

A Christmas Carol (the Deleted Scene)

Ebenezer Scrooge had been asleep for no more than a few minutes when a wrapping sound began to echo in the recesses of his chambers. Scrooge did not hear the ruckus at first. But again it came, now louder. Then closer. And louder still.

A moment later a Spirit, glowing an unearthly white, floated eerily at the foot of Scrooge's bed.

"Ebenezer Scrooge," bellowed the ghost.

Scrooge opened his eyes and knew at once that this was not a dream. He sat up slowly and found before him a Spirit who looked no taller than a boy, but reached almost to the ceiling as it floated.

"Are you the Spirit, sir, whose coming was foretold to me?" asked Scrooge.

"I am," replied the ghost.

"By what name shall I call you?"

"I am the Ghost of Christmas Future Perfect."

Scrooge stared at the ghost.

"I'm sorry. Did you say the 'Ghost of Christmas Future'?"

"No, Ebenezer, I said that I am the 'Ghost of Christmas Future *Perfect*,'" replied the Spirit, in a most ominous tone.

Now Scrooge, being a man of considerable education, knew immediately that this apparition was of a less-common conjugation, one which employed helping verbs of some sort; still, he could not remember the tense's rudiments.

"I see," replied Ebenezer, trying to conceal his ignorance.

The Spirit moved closer. "Do you know why I am here?"

Scrooge thought for a moment. "To offer me, Spirit, some glimpse of what is to come?"

The ghost hovered for a moment, and peered at Ebenezer. "No. That is incorrect. I am here, Ebenezer Scrooge, to show you what *shall have happened* to you on a Christmas that will have passed at some point in the future."

"Ah, yes, of course. Right," replied Scrooge.

The Spirit continued. "You shall see after certain future things have happened, what will have become of you after that."

Scrooge let out a sigh. He was confused. "What does that mean, good Spirit?"

"Well," said the Spirit, who was now starting to look uncomfortable. He had hoped Scrooge would not ask such a question, for the Spirit himself was not quite certain of the tense's particulars.

"It means that I am going to show you...the, uh...it's not important right now. Just come with me." And with that, he began to float in a more authoritative, ghoulish manner. "Now follow me," he moaned.

"Oh, Ghost of Christmas Future Perfect, I fear what you shall have shown me by the time we have returned tonight," Scrooge replied, trying his best to show the Spirit that he was grammatically savvy.

"We must make haste," said the Spirit, wanting to just get going already, and not dwell on the grammar.

Scrooge put on his slippers and braced himself, and the Ghost of Christmas Future Perfect guided him silently to the window.

"Where, Ghost, are you taking me?"

"We shall have seen soon enough, Ebenezer," whispered the ghost. Then the Spirit stopped and started to check his pockets.

"Damn," said the ghost quietly to himself. "I could swear I had my notes with me."

"Oh, Spirit, tell me that I shall not have been horrified by what I might discover that I shall have been doing when—"

"Just cool it for a sec, all right? I can't find my notes and this is a very complicated declension I have to deal with here. So, just give me a sec. All right?"

The ghost shook his bright, glowing head in frustration and then howled, "I can't find my notes. They're not here. To try and wing this would be a huge mistake. I mean, we could end up in the Conditional or Present Progressive, and that would be a total disaster." He paused, composed himself, and then said in a chilling tone, "I shall have been back by the time you've seen your future."

The Spirit turned and left, cursing to himself. The last thing Scrooge heard was the Spirit muttering, "This is what I get for killing a French teacher" to himself. Confused and a little relieved, Scrooge went back to bed, and the Ghost of Christmas Future Perfect never returned.

WED

5 AM: ZZZZZZ

6 AM: BZZ, BZZ, BZZ

7 AM: VO5 + H_2O
BVDs, 501s
DKNY, H&M

8 AM: TV (HD & LCD, btw): CBS, NBC, etc.
CNN: NASDAQ, NYSE

9 AM: OJ
McDLT

10 AM: SUV
CD: U2
55 MPH...BMX! OMG!...OK

11 AM: MTG w/CPA
RE: IRS...I.O.U.
I.O.U.?!...F.U., IRS!

12 PM: BLT, V8, M&M's
WC—ASAP...#2, P.U. (IBS)

1 PM: DMV

2 PM: DMV

3 PM: DMV…BS! WTF!
         (PO'D)

4 PM: Dr. (MD)
         STD?…Y/N?…N. OK

5 PM: UPS: COD
         RE: PSP
         (VIA QVC)

6 PM: YMCA—Abs, Pecs

7 PM: DVDS: XXX
         (TNA, S & M, etc.)

8 PM: KFC, 7UP
         TCBY

9 PM: CVS, ATM
         SUV: BQE → BKLN
         $200: LSD, PCP

10 PM: RSVP'd, DJ, VIP's, BYOB
         DJ: 80s (OK)
         LPs (e.g., INXS, XTC, etc.)

11 PM: MGD, MGD, MGD, MGD
         POV: MILF, WASP, 34DD
         MILF's BF: XL SOB (MOFO)
         SOL

12 AM: FUBAR
         b/c PCP, LSD, RX…

1 AM: OD

911: SOS!
NYPD, EMT, CPR

2 AM: ER…
DOA

3 AM: R.I.P.

The Middle.

Fruit Vendor
(Diary Excerpts)

Dear Diary,

After years of working for other people, tomorrow I will officially become a fruit vendor. My license came in the mail this morning and I finished stocking the stand with fruit this afternoon. I'm excited, although it is a little scary to think about just how much I have invested in this. Still, I believe that it will all be worth it. Linda thinks so too.

———

Dear Diary,

What a great first day! First I sold some oranges to a woman who was on her way to work. Then, by lunchtime I was really busy. I am officially in business!

———

Dear Diary,

It's been an amazing first week. Selling fruit definitely suits me. I can't believe I didn't do this sooner.

Dear Diary,

Something truly terrible happened today. As I was bagging some grapes for one of my neighborhood regulars, I heard a screeching sound. When I turned around to see what it was, a car came speeding down the street. It was being chased by a police car. Before I knew what happened, both of the cars drove directly into my fruit stand. The stand was completely destroyed. There was fruit everywhere. I am still in shock about what happened.

———

Dear Diary,

I managed to repair the fruit stand with some plywood and old 2 × 4s I found in my garage. It took me hours to rebuild it, but I finally got it done with Linda's help and moral support. I reopened the stand this morning. This has been quite an ordeal.

———

Dear Diary,

I cannot believe what I am about to write, but my fruit stand was knocked over again today by a car chase. It's been less than a week since the first car chase destroyed my fruit stand. I'm not exactly sure what's going on, but after I rebuild the stand I am going to find a new location for it.

———

Dear Diary,

My new location feels a lot safer. A lot of my regular customers have found me and business is booming. Strawberries are in season, and people are buying lots of them. It feels good to be selling fruit again and to have all of the craziness behind me. Linda has been so supportive through all of this.

———

Dear Diary,

Guess what happened this afternoon? A police car, involved in a high-speed chase, drove directly into my fruit stand. I'm not kidding. I almost lost it when I saw some of my beautiful strawberries smeared on the curb.

———

Dear Diary,

Another day, another car chase. I'm starting to think they're aiming for the fruit stand or something. I realized today that I have spent more time rebuilding my stand than selling fruit from it. Linda wants me to get rid of the fruit stand, but I told her I'm not a quitter. Also, I started drinking again.

———

Dear Diary,

After another two cars plowed into my fruit stand, I went down to the police precinct today and spoke with several people there about the car-chase epidemic. They told me they had more important "police work" to attend to. Can you believe that? If I see another car chase, I swear to God I am going to kill someone. I'm serious.

———

Dear Diary,

Today a jogger ran by the fruit stand and accidentally knocked a couple of apples off of it, which wasn't such a big deal. But then, while I was picking up the apples, a car chase destroyed the fruit stand. I ran after the cars until I collapsed. When Linda picked me up from the hospital, we had another fight about the fruit stand.

———

Dear Diary,

This afternoon, when I was trying to move my car to a better parking spot, I accidentally drove it directly into my fruit stand really fast. In a sick way, it felt kind of good. I'm starting to feel a little unstable. Linda told me I should see a psychiatrist. I laughed in her face and then started to cry. Whatever, I need to get back to rebuilding the stand now.

———

Dear Diary,

I'm having serious doubts about the fruit stand. And my recurring car-chase nightmares are getting more intense. I went to see Grandpa yesterday. I thought maybe he could offer some advice, seeing as how he used to be a fruit vendor himself. When I said the words "fruit stand" to him he started to shake and got a crazy look in his eyes. Then he ran into his kitchen and hid in one of the cabinets. I don't remember what happened after that because I was too drunk.

———

Dear Diary,

Yesterday I sold the fruit stand. Today I was on my way to deliver it to its new owner when a police car drove directly into it. I started laughing really hard and drooling, and then I couldn't stop laughing. Someone said that before I passed out I began to "scream and wrestle with the fruit." I honestly don't really remember doing that or writing the manifesto, which I apparently e-mailed to everyone I know. What a crazy few months it has been. Also, Linda left me.

Dear Diary,

I don't ever want to see another piece of fruit again. On a lighter note, I spoke to my friend Dave today. He's looking for someone to partner with him in a new business venture. We are going to start a mirror-moving company. I'm looking forward to a fresh start. I believe this investment will prove to be a good one.

Pets (a Conversation)

I had a conversation with an alien from outer space. I don't remem-
ber much of it. I was on a camping trip with my friends and I
couldn't sleep, so I went for a walk. I started to wander through the
woods and that's all I really remember. At some point I must have
sat on my phone and accidentally called my friend's phone because
part of my conversation ended up in his voicemail as a very long
message . . .

ME: . . . and that's where babies come from.
ALIEN: I see.
ME: I still can't believe I'm talking to a real, live alien! Wow!
    Can I take your picture?
ALIEN: No. Calm down. Drink this.

[*Drinking sounds*]

ME: I feel weird. What did I just drink?
ALIEN: I have another question.
ME: Okay.
ALIEN: What are pets?
ME: Pets. Oh, that's easy. A pet is an animal that a person has.

ALIEN: Why?

ME: What?

ALIEN: Why does the person have the animal?

ME: Um, well, because they want to have a friend that's an animal.

ALIEN: I see. So, the person and the animal are friends?

ME: Yeah.

ALIEN: Does the animal, then, also have the person?

ME: Uh...No. The animal is the pet, so the person *has* the animal, you know, as a pet. That's what makes it a "pet." So, where are you from anyway?

ALIEN: That is not important.

ME: This is awesome! Can I take your picture?

ALIEN: No. Calm down. Drink this.

[*Drinking sounds*]

ME: I feel weird. What did I just drink?

ALIEN: Now, do animals have pets?

ME: No.

ALIEN: So, only humans *have* other animals. Hm. Can these "pets" come and go as they please?

ME: No, they can't.

ALIEN: Why not?

ME: Because then they would get away.

ALIEN: So a pet is a prisoner.

ME: Well, no, not exactly—

ALIEN: Ah, it is a hostage then?

ME: Well, I guess technically you could say that, but the pet isn't captured—well, it can be, but I think—I mean, it depends on the type of pet, so I don't know if you could really call it a "hostage."

ALIEN: Well, does the pet have a choice?

ME: No, not really.

ALIEN: That's a hostage.

ME: I think it's different, because—

ALIEN: Can the pet eat whenever it wants?

ME: No.

ALIEN: That sounds a lot like a hostage to me.

ME: . . .

ALIEN: When does the pet eat?

ME: That's up to the owner.

ALIEN: "Owner"?

ME: Yeah, the person is the owner of the pet.

ALIEN: I thought they were friends.

ME: They are. They're friends, but one of them owns the other one and feeds him and trains him to go to the bathroom at certain times and to behave certain ways.

ALIEN: Hm.

ME: Also, the owner can make the pet cuddle with him whenever he wants and will sometimes dress up the pet, like on Halloween.

ALIEN: I see . . . What is Halloween?

ME: Wow! This is crazy. I can't believe I'm talking to an alien!! Can I take your picture?

ALIEN: No. Calm down. Drink more of this.

ME: I don't really want to.

ALIEN: Drink this.

ME: Okay.

[*Drinking Sounds*]

ALIEN: Now, what is Halloween?

A Cappella Group Freak Accidents

An a cappella group is singing out on the quad of a college campus. Suddenly, a grizzly bear, which has just escaped from a nearby zoo, emerges from some bushes and charges directly into the group. The bear mauls several members of the a cappella group, attacking, with especially gruesome ferocity, one of the male baritones, who has a penchant for performing "funny" skits between songs. Animal control specialists arrive a short time later and restrain the bear. Paramedics do their best to treat the badly injured a cappella singers. Both the paramedics and animal control specialists are secretly pleased.

———

While an a cappella group is walking down the street and singing to themselves at a volume that is loud enough for everyone around them to hear, a passing fire truck inexplicably malfunctions. The fire truck's hoses spontaneously turn on and blast the members of the group, knocking the singers off their feet and into some nearby bushes, which happen to be poison ivy. As the water hits the poison ivy, it creates a poison-ivy mist, which the singers inhale, giving them poison ivy on their vocal cords. The firemen turn off the hoses and drive away. They are secretly pleased.

An a cappella group is practicing in the hallway of a college dormitory. Their "cute" renditions of several old Motown hits cause a nearby swarm of bees to become insanely agitated. The aggravated bees enter the hallway and engulf the a cappella group, stinging each of the singers repeatedly. This commotion disturbs a hornets' nest located just outside a nearby window. The hornets fly in moments later and attack the already badly bloated bodies of the a cappella group's members. Hours later, after smoke is pumped into the hallway to clear out the bees and hornets, nurses from the campus infirmary enter the corridor and treat the badly stung singers. The nurses are secretly pleased.

———

Several a cappella groups are onstage together at the annual "Spring Sing" concert. In the middle of performing their best ironic medley of 80's songs, the stage suddenly collapses under the weight of the singers. The a cappella groups immediately fall down and roll off into a large pile. A moment later, the elaborate lighting rig that is hanging from the rafters above them spontaneously unfastens and crashes down onto the pile of singers. The heat from the lights sparks the frayed wires and ignites the pile, causing all of the groups to burst into flames. The crowd is secretly pleased.

———

An a cappella group is in the middle of singing an unrequested encore in front of a captive Parents' Weekend audience. A moment later a small meteor, about the exact size of an a cappella group, crashes through the roof of the auditorium and flies directly into the a cappella group just as they begin to perform their "instrumental" version of "Mr. Sandman." Several members of the group are instantly pulverized by the meteor as others explode into little bits, which shoot off into the far corners of the room. The audience is stunned...and also secretly pleased.

———————

An a cappella group performs and somehow manages not to irritate anyone. Everyone is secretly confused.

My Checks

What I imagine my dolphin-themed personal checks do for me.

Two landlords are reviewing my rental application:

—So who should we rent the apartment to?

—I'm not sure. This woman has excellent credit, a stable job, great references, and she is willing to pay an extra month's rent up front.

—She sounds great.

—She's also an interior designer and has some excellent ideas on how to improve the space.

—Wow.

—But, on the other hand, there's this guy. He doesn't have a steady job. He's got lousy credit, and his application looks pretty messy. I think there's a food stain on it.

—Hm.

—But...take a look at his personal checks. They have dolphins on them. Look at these dolphins! They are so friendly and likable.

—Let me see that check...Wow, this is great! I love his

dolphin-themed personal checks. They just have so much personality!

—They really do. I think his checks say a lot about him.

—I think so, too. I'd say, based on his checks, he is clearly the more likable candidate.

—Yep. Especially when you compare his checks to hers.

—Let me see her checks…Yikes. Hers are just the standard-issue yellow checks—so unimaginative and impersonal. I don't think I want someone like that living in the apartment.

—Well, I definitely don't want someone cold like that in our place. I want a tenant who's got some heart, like the dolphin guy. It's really no contest.

—I agree. Dolphin guy wins.

—Hey, do you think we should maybe also give him a break on the rent?

—*(Looks at dolphin check again. Smiles and nods.)* Definitely.

A guy I paid with a check is talking to his friend:

—You know, I was going to cash this guy's check, but I don't want to.

—Why?

—Because I really like looking at the check.

—Let me see that. *(Looks at check.)* …Dolphins. Wow! That is really cool.

—Yeah.

—That check is indeed very nice to look at. The dolphins are very appealing. The whole scene is warm and friendly.

—I know. I was thinking that I might not cash it.

—I can see why. I don't blame you. I mean, looking at the check is almost worth more than cashing it, if you ask me.

—Yeah. You're right. I'm going to put it up on my corkboard and never cash it. I think any guy who likes dolphins so much that he's willing to express it in his business transactions can just keep the money as far as I'm concerned.

—I was going to say the same thing. Good decision.

—Thanks. I feel good about it.

I am talking to a woman just after getting into a minor car accident with her:

—Again, I am so sorry for the damage to your car. Can I write you a check to cover it?

—Um...I think I should call my insurance company.

—Are you sure? I've got my checkbook right here. (*I take out my checkbook and open to a blank dolphin-themed check.*) Tell you what, why don't I write you a check, and if the damages end up costing more than—

—Wait. (*She looks at the check.*)...Are those dolphins on your checks?

—Uh, yes. Yes they are.

—Awww. That is so cute. You know, I *love* dolphins. (*She smiles.*) I was once stranded in the middle of the ocean and a pack of dolphins that looked just like those saved my life.

—Wow. Really?

—Yeah. You seem like a sweet guy.

—Well, thank you. I like these checks because they remind me that it's important to live life with grace and enthusiasm...kind of like a dolphin, I guess.

—(*She looks at me and smiles.*) Hey...how about we forget about the whole car situation and you just take me to lunch instead?

—Really?

—Yes, really. I would love to have lunch with you.

—Okay, I think that would be nice. But wait, weren't you on your way to work?

—Oh I was, but it's no big deal. I'm a model. They can just reschedule the photo shoot.

—Well then great. Let's get some lunch.

—Also, I know this is a little forward, but do you mind if I kiss you?

—Not at all.

A Crossword Puzzle

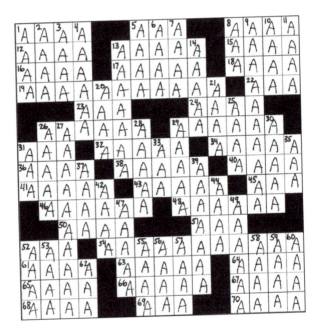

ACROSS

1. Two batteries.
5. Popular organization for car owners.
8. Said when trying to get someone's attention.
12. American Association of Advertising Agencies, abbr.
13. Key chains owned by April, Alexis, Andrea, and Amelia.
15. Prefix used to procure a good spot in the Yellow Pages.
16. Found on an American Airlines' airplane tail wing (both sides).
17. An opera singer's vanity plate?
18. Two sets of souvenir sweatbands from Anaheim.
19. Expression of pain.
22. Minor league baseball league classification.
23. France's credit rating.
24. Mirror image of 16 Across.
26. A very good report card.
29. A group of female gymnasts' bra cup sizes.
31. Sold with 69 Across.
32. Something Fonzie might say.
34. A very boring chord progression.
36. Four children's refrigerator magnets.
38. Sweatshirts of five fans at an Auburn football game.
40. A lame graffiti tag?
41. Someone with a bad stutter trying to say "Aardvark."
43. Board of Health ratings of last five restaurants I ate in.
45. American Accounting Association, abbr.
46. A bunch of a certain guitar string.
48. Sound heard when an obsessive child plays with a Speak & Spell.
50. First letter of Greek, Roman, Spanish, and English alphabets.
51. Uncommon fraternity name.
52. Stadium section that is high up.
54. What appears when a certain key on a computer keyboard sticks.

61. Sound of someone starting to say the alphabet in a cave.
63. Five indefinite articles.
64. American Association of Anesthesiology Assistants, abbr.
65. One way to jump four octaves.
66. What it sounds like when trying to pluck 46 Across.
67. Some white piano keys.
68. Anagram of 5 Across.
69. Type of battery used in many TV remotes.
70. Homophone of "foray"?

DOWN
1. Best grades of milk, beef, eggs, and yogurt.
2. First letter of first four states, alphabetically.
3. Four Rolodex tabs from four different Rolodexes.
4. Overheard in a dentist's office.
5. 43690, in hexadecimal.
6. A strange thing to teach a parrot to say.
7. Found in a spoon while eating Alphabits cereal.
8. Angels', Diamond Backs', Braves' hats.
9. All of the vowels from a famous palindrome about a famous canal.
10. What it might look like as a letter is falling off a sign.
11. Authentication, Authorization, Accounting, and Auditing (remote access security approach that controls network access), for short.
13. Portion of SAT answer sheet from person who did not do well on test.
14. What audiences gave a guy onstage the last five times he asked for it.
20. Lower Merion Little League division for players who are 11 years old as of April 30th.
21. Heard as person in 41 Across continues to struggle.
25. Part of "Hey Jude."
26. Excerpt from notebook of child learning how to write.

27. One way to write the phone number (222) 222-2222.
28. All of the vowels in a magician's favorite word?
29. First characters of five adjacent parking spaces, located on the first level of a parking structure.
30. A lazy password.
31. 22 Across, backwards.
33. __-line dress, __-line coat, __-line haircut.
35. High-score holder in numerous arcade games.
37. Found on piece of paper, in wastebasket, in Calligraphy class.
39. A bunch of window seats on an airplane.
42. Items found in a rubber stamp kit.
44. "La La La La," in Solflege, C Major.
47. Found on five of Hester Prynne's outfits?
49. Unlikely hand in Scrabble.
52. Strong rating for cultured pearls.
53. Elicited during a foot rub.
55. The not famous, but actual "_____ Hotelwelt Kuebler" hotel in Karlsruhe, Germany.
56. 13 Down minus 31 Across.
57. Albany Area Amateur Astronomers, abbr.
58. Sound you might hear if "A Hard Day's Night" skips on the third word in the song.
59. Every other letter in the 22nd state.
60. Opening Morse code signal sent in order to get receiver's attention.
62. What one might say when viewing this puzzle.

Sheila

George was drunk. He wobbled on the surface of the frozen lake. He had been drinking a lot lately. It started shortly after Lori left. After being together for only a few months, George had asked Lori to move in with him. She told him she wanted to see the world. George told her he loved her. She said she thought things were moving too fast. Then George went and got her name tattooed on his leg. When he showed Lori the tattoo, she cried and kissed him. The next day she left to see the world. That was four months ago.

Standing there on the lake with his buddies, drinking vodka out of a red plastic cup, George tried not to think about Lori. But it was no use. Today was the three-week anniversary of the last time he spoke to her. Lori had called collect from India that day, from a small village just outside of Varanasi. The phone connection was bad and the conversation was short.

"I miss you," said George.

"I just shaved my head," Lori replied. "I think my spirit animal is a caribou."

"Oh." George was happy to hear her voice, even with the bad connection. It made her sound like she was floating in space or something. And she might as well have been. India was a world away.

"When do you think you'll be back?" George asked, trying not to sound too desperate.

"Um..." Lori replied, "Ooh, I've got to run. We're about to burn one of the elders' bodies! I'll catch you later."

George just couldn't accept that the relationship was over. He was holding on to something that was no longer there, and everyone but George could see it. He'd even had the tattoo of her name underlined, hoping the added emphasis would somehow help him rekindle things with Lori. Of course, it didn't. It only made it look like George had the title of a book on his leg. People would look at his leg and say, "Who's the author?"

George's friends were worried about him. He was drunk more frequently these days. And he wasn't a good drunk. Some people become talkers when they're drunk. Others become huggers. When George got drunk, he became a tackler. After a few drinks he'd get that crazy look in his eyes and start to rock back and forth. That's when anyone standing near him knew it was time to move out of the way or find something sturdy to stand behind.

So, that afternoon, as George charged across the ice, his buddy, Owen, calmly stepped behind a tree. George barreled past him and careened off the tree. Then, with all the grace of an injured water buffalo, George crashed through the ice.

When the paramedics fished George out of the ice, he was unconscious and blue. They rushed him to the hospital, where he died just after 8 pm.

Emerging from total blackness, George found himself suddenly standing on a boat in a warm, sun-drenched place, moving gently toward a coastline. There were other people with him on the boat, most of them were older. The boat was overflowing with passengers, all crowded together, all completely silent, all dead. George didn't know if this was Heaven, but he knew it wasn't Earth. It's too "glowy," he thought. He knew he was dead, because when you're dead, you just know it. It's like stepping in gum. As soon as it happens, there is no question about what it is.

As strange as it all felt, it was also familiar and wonderful at the same time. George felt warm and serene, and relieved, kind of like the way you feel right after you sneeze or take off some ski boots, but even more so. And he wasn't drunk or even a little bit hungover. He checked his breath. It didn't smell like beer or vodka but more like strawberries. George hadn't eaten any strawberries. He knew this was a special place.

There was no tunnel or relatives, or pearly gates, just some strange people waving at George and the other recently departed folks arriving with him. Rolling hills stretched out into the distance behind the friendly-looking people who stood on the shoreline. As the boat floated toward the waiting crowd, George spotted a couple of angels, who, on closer inspection, looked more like some guys wearing tattered angel costumes. Still, this was more beautiful than any place George had ever seen. Of course, he had spent most of his life in New Jersey, so that's not saying much.

George scanned the faces of the waiting people. Every one of them emanated kindness. Although, a couple of them had an expression like "Do I know you? Oh, I don't... well, I'm disappointed, but welcome anyway."

One of these faces seemed to glow brighter than the others. It was the face of a woman. From the moment he saw her, George couldn't stop looking at her. Unlike the other people who were waiting there, she seemed to be walking by. When she saw George, she stopped and smiled at him. They gazed at each other unselfconsciously. Then one of the angel guys floated in front of her face, blocking her view of George. She batted the angel away. The angel looked annoyed about it. She kind of told him off as he floated away. Then she looked back at George and smiled. He smiled back.

George walked through the crowd and made his way to the woman. When he got to her, he didn't know what to say. He was mesmerized by her beauty, and also a little jet-lagged from dying.

"Pretty annoying angel, huh?" said George.

"Yeah." She laughed. "They're not angels. They're just guys

dressed up like them. They're here to help people make the transition after they've, uh…"

"Died?"

"Yeah. Sorry. I didn't know if you knew."

"I figured I was dead when I went to scratch my arm and my hand went through it."

She laughed again. "I guess that's a good clue."

"I'm George."

"Sheila."

They shook hands. The moment they touched George felt a spark like nothing he'd ever felt before. This must be what they mean when they say "love at first sight," thought George. He had never felt so connected so quickly to anyone before, ever. George knew that he had found his soul mate, and she was hot.

As Sheila spoke, her words floated like notes plucked from a harp, a really good harp. She was in the middle of telling George about her cat when her voice started to sound distorted, like from the Doppler effect or something. The light around George started to dim and he felt a pulling sensation. A moment later Sheila and everything else around her began receding, and then suddenly it all disappeared into darkness. George felt heavy and sluggish. It got very cold. Pain shot through his body. He tossed and turned and then opened his eyes.

"We got him!" shouted a doctor.

"We've got a pulse," added one of the nurses.

The heart monitor began jumping. The doctors and nurses celebrated. Their persistence had paid off. George coughed. The bright light of the O.R. spilled into his eyes. He squinted and passed out.

The next day George woke up in a hospital bed. He found a doctor sitting next to him, a short man with very thick eyebrows.

"Hello, George," said the doctor. "How are you feeling?" As he spoke, the doctor's eyebrows moved gently up and down, like well-trained caterpillars.

"Where am I?" asked George.

The doctor told George that he had been dead for almost five minutes the day before. The icy water had made it possible for them to revive him.

"You're a lucky man, George," said the doctor. "You're going to be fine."

"Where's Sheila?" asked George.

"Who?"

"Wait, you mean, I'm not dead?" George whined.

"No. You're alive." The doctor flashed a warm smile. "We saved you."

"Oh," said George. He was visibly disappointed.

The doctor's smile vanished. "You're welcome," he muttered as he stood up and left the room. "...prick."

Two days later George was released from the hospital. He still couldn't believe he had died. He'd never even had the flu before, let alone death. He felt lucky, but he was confused. He wanted to see Sheila again.

George's friends threw him a surprise party. It was a "Resurrection Party." Everyone showed up, many dressed as disciples. The party made George feel kind of uncomfortable, especially when they brought out the cake and he had to eat his own "blood and body." Still he was relieved to see his friends, and for the first time in months, he had totally forgotten about Lori.

About a week later, George sat in his therapist's office and opened up about his recent, temporary death.

"It's just my luck," George complained. "I finally manage to find my soul mate, but it happens only *after* I die. And then I can't even stay dead once I've found her."

"You were dead for five minutes, George. That's not a basis for a relationship," countered his therapist.

"You weren't there. You don't know."

"George, this is your typical pattern. You claim you want to be in a committed relationship, but you always fall for women you can't have. Remember the Japanese tourist you met at the airport? Then there was the newlywed you saw leaving the church. And then Lori, who always told you she wanted to travel. And now this Sheila, who is either dead or worse, imaginary."

"She is not imaginary!"

"Either way, it's unhealthy. You need to forget about her and try to date someone who is available and alive. Stop worrying about finding a soul mate and just try to find a date."

Sheila was eating lunch with her best friend, Erin. They'd been friends since death.

"What were you doing at Arrivals?" Erin asked.

Arrivals was typically where dead spouses and random opportunists hung out, waiting to be reunited with the recently deceased or to sell them maps to homes of the dead stars.

"I was just walking by. I was running errands in the area."

"So this guy just happened to be arriving as you walked by?"

"Yeah. It was really romantic. We made eye contact, and the next thing I knew we were deep in conversation. He was really sweet and just . . . *different* than a lot of the guys up here."

"What do you mean?"

"I don't know, he just seemed so . . ."—Sheila searched for the words—". . . so full of life."

Erin laughed. "Well, that's no surprise. The guy had just died. I know it's charming, but let me tell you, that doesn't last. I once dated a guy who'd just died. At first it was great. But then, after a couple of months, the novelty of it wore off, and then he was just another dead guy like every other guy around here."

"But this was different."

Erin could see how excited Sheila was, so she tried to seem interested. "So, then what happened?" she asked.

"Well, we were talking and laughing, really connecting, and then out of nowhere he started to float backwards. And then he was gone."

"Oh," Erin replied.

"What do you mean 'Oh'?"

"I mean 'Oh' as in 'Oh, he's gone.' They took him back."

Sheila looked puzzled.

"Back to his life," explained Erin.

"What?"

"I'm sorry to tell you this, sweetie, but this George guy is back on Earth. You won't see him again until he dies again."

Sheila didn't want to believe it, but she knew Erin was right. Erin knew a lot about life. She had been obsessed with it ever since she died.

Sheila was disappointed. She really liked George. And, even though they had only spoken for a few minutes, she knew they had real chemistry. But she also knew there was no way to date a living person, so she tried to forget about George and get on with the rest of her afterlife.

About a week later, Sheila's phone rang.

"Hello?"

"Hi. Is Sheila there?"

"This is Sheila. Who's this?"

"My name is Stew. I work over in Visitation. I understand you're interested in someone on Earth."

"Well, um, yes, I was. I mean I guess I am but…wait, how did you get my number?"

"I'm a friend of Larry's. He is seeing your friend Dianne. Erin told her about your recent encounter. I think I can help you."

The next day Sheila met Stew for coffee. He explained that if she really wanted to see George, she could visit him on Earth by obtaining a visa.

"How do I get a visa?" asked Sheila.

"Well, there are two options. The first is reincarnation. I don't recommend that though, because it's risky. You could end up as a lizard or a dog or some sort of insect. Plus, even if you're lucky enough to become a person, there will be a pretty big age difference to deal with once you get there."

"What's the other option?"

Stew took a sip of his coffee. "The other option is that you go as a ghost."

Sheila thought for a moment. She wanted to see George again, but as a ghost? "Ghosts are scary," she thought. "And on top of that, I'm not a night person." On the other hand, dating had not been going well. And she couldn't stop thinking about George.

Stew continued. "All you need is some unfinished business. I can help you submit a proper request, and then, if it's approved, you'll be able to visit Earth as a ghost with an unfinished business visa."

"Hm," said Sheila. "Well, what qualifies as unfinished business?"

"Unfinished business is usually solving a murder or helping to solve a murder, or ... well, it's pretty much just stuff involving murders."

"I see," said Sheila, disappointed. "I guess I don't qualify then."

"Well, not necessarily. That's where I can help you. I have a friend in the department. He can put together the paperwork. It'll take some favors, but if you've got the money, I think I can get you that visa."

Two weeks later George was brushing his teeth when he heard a strange noise. He figured it was the wind and shrugged it off. Then it came again. He walked into his living room. There, next to his coffee table, he saw a strange light shooting around the room.

"Hellooooo, George," said the light, trying its best not to sound spooky.

"Oh my God," said George. "What do you want?"

"It's meeee, Sheila," replied the ghost.

George looked closer. It was Sheila. She looked different, more see-through and kind of pale, but it was her.

"Jesus. What happened to you? Are you okay?"

"Yeeeeees, George, I'm fine. I'm a ghost. I came to visit youuuuuu."

"Wow. Sheila. I thought I'd never see you again."

"Meeee toooo," she replied.

George invited Sheila to sit down, and she did her best to, floating just above the chair. They started to talk, picking up right where they'd left off, connecting in the same effortless way they had done two weeks earlier.

Despite her initial ghoulish appearance, Sheila looked great. She explained that those longer vowels that rang out when she spoke were not intentional. It was a side effect of being a ghost.

"It's sort of built into the ghost speech mechanism," she explained. "I guess to make haunting easier."

With a little practice, Sheila was able to minimize the effect. Although, every now and then she would say "boo" without warning. George took it in stride. They talked and laughed and shared stories all night. And before they knew it, it was morning. As the sun rose, George walked Sheila to the door.

"I had so much fun tonight," Sheila said, glowing demurely.

"Me toooooo," responded George.

Sheila laughed.

"When can I see you again?" asked George.

"Well, tomorrow I have to visit some people involved with a murder, because of my visa, but I'm free the next night."

"Great," said George. "It's a date."

Two nights later, Sheila was back in George's apartment. Again, they stayed up talking, hours passing like minutes, each of them finishing each other's sentences. George made tea for Sheila. It went right through her. They laughed about it. Then Sheila inhabited one of George's throw pillows and danced around with it. She challenged him to a pillow fight. As they jousted with pillows they had trouble catching their breath from laughing so hard, and also, in Sheila's case, from being inside a pillow.

Sheila came by every night for the next week. And every night she and George stayed up and explored their own magical little world. Nothing else seemed to matter.

George asked Sheila to be his girlfriend. She said yes. And that night they kissed for the first time. It took a little bit of effort, but they managed to do it.

At first George didn't tell anyone about Sheila. He knew people would have trouble understanding. But he couldn't hide his happiness. He was falling in love and he needed to tell someone.

"I'm seeing Sheila," he told his therapist.

"Sheila? What do you mean?"

"You remember Sheila. I met her when I was dead. She's been visiting me, as a ghost."

His therapist sighed. "George, do you really believe you're dating a ghost?"

"*Dating* a ghost? I'm sleeping with her."

George's therapist choked on his Diet Sprite. "What are you talking about?"

"Well, she floats on top of me, and—"

"Okay," interrupted his therapist. "You know what? I think we should just leave it there."

"But—"

"Sorry, George. It looks like we're out of time," he said with a concerned look in his eye and a little bit of soda in his beard. "I'm not really qualified to deal with this sort of thing. Try to get some rest."

George knew he wasn't crazy, but judging from his therapist's reaction, he decided it would be best to keep his relationship with Sheila to himself for a while.

Sheila continued to visit George, usually at night. That was the best time to do so. He had to work days at his ad job, and it was a lot easier for him to see her at night, literally, because of the luminescence of her ghost body. Sheila split her time between seeing him and visiting people related to the murder case. She had to make sure she stayed involved with the case or she risked being discovered by the Visa Department. It was a complicated case, which was a mixed blessing for Sheila. On the one hand, it ensured that she'd be able to stay on Earth for a while. On the other hand, it was getting tedious. Every time she haunted someone who was involved with the murder case, she had to deal with their typical, incredulous reactions to meeting a ghost, and then she'd have to answer a littany of questions about the homicide. She tried not to let it bother her, reminding herself that it was worth it to be with George. But it was starting to wear on her.

The next few months were the happiest of George's life. He had found the perfect woman. She was smart, beautiful, sexy, and fun. And at the same time, she didn't cramp his style. He still had his days to himself and plenty of nights to go out with his buddies when Sheila was off haunting a detective or visiting a witness.

Halloween was spectacular. George threw a big party. Everyone came. Sheila was a hit. It was a great way to ease his friends into meeting her. A couple of his more skeptical friends couldn't see Sheila at first, but soon everyone met her and warmed up to her. As George's friends started to know and accept Sheila, he started to think about asking her to be his wife.

Then, one afternoon, George heard a knock on his front door. When he opened the door, he found a man standing there with a somber look on his face.

"Hello. Are you George?"

"Yes, how can I help you?"

George had a bad feeling about this. He wondered if this man was one of the detectives Sheila had been haunting. Had something happened?

"I'm Mark."

"Hi, Mark. What is this about?"

Mark sighed and looked at George. "I'm Sheila's husband."

George froze. He didn't know what to say. "Are you a ghost?" asked George.

"No."

"Oh." George didn't know if he should feel better or worse. He invited Mark in to talk.

They sat down at the kitchen table.

"Sheila never told me she was married," explained George.

"I'm not surprised," Mark replied.

George fixed Mark a drink and grabbed a club soda for himself. George was no longer drinking, thanks to Sheila. As Mark talked about Sheila and their marriage, George listened closely. But he was feeling so many emotions at once, it was hard for him to concentrate.

"How did you find me?" George asked.

"Well, I get in touch with Sheila from time to time, you know, through a psychic. The last few times I tried to contact her, one of her dead friends answered, saying things like 'Oh, she just stepped out' or 'sorry, you just missed her!'"

George was still in shock. Mark continued.

"So, I started to get suspicious and asked my psychic if he could find out anything for me. For a little extra money he went through some of Sheila's stuff, and—"

George interrupted. "Wait, 'Went through some of her stuff'? You mean, up there?"

"Yeah," Mark replied. "He's a very good psychic. Anyway, when he was going through her stuff he found your name and address."

George stared at his kitchen table and tried to digest everything Mark had told him.

"God, I don't know what to say. I'm ... I'm sorry."

"Listen," said Mark, "I'm not telling you what to do or anything. I just thought you should know what the situation was. I mean, it's not like Sheila and I are still living together, obviously, but I still do have feelings for her, and as far as I could tell, we were still working things out."

A few minutes later they shook hands and Mark left. George was devastated. "How could this be?" he thought. "Why hadn't she said anything?" George sat on his couch and stared at the wall until he fell asleep.

George awoke to find Sheila floating next to him on the couch. She was tired from visiting the brother-in-law of the murder victim. He always asked her difficult questions about the case and usually tried to photograph her. It always put her in a bad mood.

George felt uneasy. He couldn't look at Sheila. She knew something was wrong.

"Is something bothering youuuuuuuuu?" she said. Her vowels still rang out from time to time, mostly when she was feeling more emotional.

"Well," said George, "I was wondering if there was anything you wanted me to know about you, about your life, maybe that you haven't told me. We never really talk about it."

"Uh, no. Nothing I can think of," Sheila responded. "There's not much to talk about really. As you know I died from an allergic reaction after eating some chili. Sometimes they put peanut butter in it, which I didn't know at the time. But I've told you that already."

George nodded. "So, nothing else, then?"

Sheila shrugged, then offered, "The most interesting things that have happened to me, happened after I died." She floated closer to George.

George looked at her. "And what about your husband?"

Sheila's face turned white, even more white than usual.

"What are you talking about?" she said.

"I'm talking about Mark."

"Mark? Uh . . . That was a long time ago," replied Sheila, trying to play it off. "I didn't think it was important."

"You didn't think it was important!? . . . I'd say being married is pretty important, Sheila! That's the kind of thing you might want to mention to someone before you start sleeping with them!"

"Mark is something from my past."

"Oh really?" replied George. "And is that why you're still in touch with him?"

"What? We talk occasionally, but just through a psychic. We're just friends. What's the big deal?"

"What's the big deal?! Are you kidding right now?!"

Sheila floated to the couch. "I don't know what Mark told you, but we're just friends. Nothing more. He's dated other people, you know. He just contacts me when he needs something."

"How can we have a relationship if you can't be honest with me?"

"*Honest* with you?!" Sheila started to lose her temper. "I became a *ghost* for you! Do you know what I've been through to make this work?"

"Oh, here we go again with the ghost stuff!" snapped George.

"*I'm* the one who went and got a visa," shouted Sheila. "*I'm* the one who left all of her friends in the Afterlife to come and be with you. Do you know what it's like to suddenly blurt out 'Boo' when you're trying to say something? Do you ever wonder what it feels like to be drawn to cemeteries? No, you don't, because you're Mr. 'Still Alive.' Well I'm the one here who has to keep visiting a murder case that she doesn't even *care about*." Her voice was trembling. "I did all of this for you!"

"I never asked you to!"

"Oh, but you never stopped me. Did you? You sure didn't seem to have any problem with it when I was floating in your bed. Did you?"

George didn't say anything.

"People told me to watch out. They said, 'George has trouble with commitment.' And I said, 'No. He's not like that. Not the George I know.' But they were right. This isn't about Mark. It's about you."

"Of course it's about Mark. You haven't been honest with me. God, I just can't look at you the same way."

"Oh come off it, George. I'm dead. Yes, Mark and I were married, okay? Yes. But have you ever heard of 'till death do us part'? Well, I died. And we parted."

She continued. "By the way, I'm not the only one here who failed to mention a relationship. When were you going to tell me about Lori?"

"How do you know about her?"

"I found out on Halloween. Your friend Andrew told me."

"Well that's over. It ended before I even met you."

"Did it? Because when I visited Lori she still seemed into you."

"You visited Lori? How could you do that?"

"I was curious. It's a free world. If it's so 'over,' then what's the big deal?"

"This is crazy. I can't believe you haunted Lori. I think you should go. And I think it would be best if…if we just…if we were just friends."

"Friends? Really? That's it. What about all that talk about being your 'Soul mate'? Was that all bullshit so you could have a fling with a ghost? Was it all just so you could have a good story? Huh? 'Hey everybody, I slept with a ghost!'"

"That's not fair, Sheila."

"You had your fun, but then it started to get too real for you. God forbid you have to actually commit to someone, George. You know what, this isn't worth it. I've jumped through so many hoops to make this work, changing myself for *you*. I had a pretty good afterlife before you came along. Goodbye, George."

Sheila turned and stormed off, creating such a supernatural ruckus that she even scared herself in the process.

Sheila returned to the Afterlife, heartbroken and exhausted. But part of her was also relieved. Being a ghost had been difficult. And with a little distance from it all she realized that George was not her soul mate, after all. He was just a cute guy who wasn't dead. Sheila returned to her friends and to the casual dating she knew so well in death. She vowed never to get involved with anyone on Earth again.

Mark tried to get in touch with Sheila a couple more times. She ignored his calls.

It took some time, but George got over Sheila. He even started dating again and found new appreciation for the pleasures of making love to living women.

Ironically, years later George and Mark would end up becoming good friends. They ran into each other at a screenwriting symposium and decided to grab lunch. They discovered that they had a lot in common. They had both worked in advertising and were both hoping to break into writing. They started to kick around ideas and then began writing together not long after that. George and Mark developed an idea for a sitcom based on their experiences with Sheila. They pitched and sold it to a major television network. The series aired. It became a hit show and ran for seven seasons.

George got married and had two children. He lived to be a wealthy old man and died peacefully one night in his sleep.

As George returned to the idyllic shores of the Afterlife, waiting for him on the other side was Sheila, along with her attorney.

Products

I like to read. I read everything: books, magazines, newspapers, pamphlets, signs, T-shirts, and just about anything else with words printed on it. Here is some prose that I found on the packaging of some everyday products.

————

"We founded Wholesome Foods in 1973 because we believed that wholesome foods come from wholesome land. And that belief has guided our company ever since. That's why every piece of Wholesome Foods produce is rubbed on a virgin before it goes into the truck. So you can be sure every bite is fresh, wholesome, and totally free of sex."

"At Hillsdale Farms we use no hormones in our turkeys. In fact, we pride ourselves on doing no harm whatsoever to our turkeys. We raise them naturally and then simply encourage our juicy, organically fed turkeys to take their own lives after they go through our patented 'depressive introspection' existential crisis."

"Yitz crackers taste great with cheese or party dip. Try them with peanut butter for a fun snack or with jam for a sweet treat. Or, try making a little hat out of them, you moron."

"This robe is provided for your comfort while staying at the Royal Clifton. If you wish to purchase one, please contact Guest Services, and then brace yourself, because we're pretty sure it costs more than your house."

"WARNING: This snorkel quickly becomes a giant straw if you're not careful."

"While we're not exactly sure what goes into our gluten-free gingersnaps, the man who brings us the snaps in his old wooden cart seems very friendly and relatively clean. And he always covers his mouth when he coughs. Either way, every bag of gingersnaps we sell meets our "golden standard of sell-ability.""

"Just as a gushing brook endlessly winds its way through a forest, our Mint Melee tea will bring the same unstoppable force to your urethra. Enjoy Mint Melee tea at home, near your bathroom. We mean it."

"Munchables are fun for the whole family. Made from 100% all-natural laboratory chemicals, these munchy, crunchy snacks are guaranteed to fill even the hungriest tummy. Make sure to drink plenty of water with Munchables to really get the party going (and to avoid stomach implosion)."

"Vitalique shampoo is infused with pro-vitamins and natural moisturizers as well as age-defying color enhancers that clean hair at its roots with a patented 3-step, dirt-defying vibrancy enhancer, leaving your hair looking and smelling fresh, young, revitalized, and rejuvenated, making it bounce and shine with reinvigorated, reinfused infusions of revitalization and pro-color vitamins and other things you need to hear in order to buy this hair soap."

"This product may contain traces of Nick."

"For over 50 years, we've used the same secret recipe. That's what makes our desserts taste so delicious. And that's all you need to know about it. And we suggest you don't go snooping around for any more information about the recipe. Others have done so at their own peril. So how about you just enjoy the shortbread and don't ask any more questions."

"OfficeZone's Clinger Adhesive Strips hold firmly and reliably. Perfect for home, school, or office. But not perfect for skin. Be careful. These strips will stick to your skin forever. That is not an exaggeration. If one of them even taps your skin, it will fuse instantly. Don't pull on it. That will make it burrow even farther into your flesh. Just leave it where it is and learn to live with it."

"Worthington Water Crackers are created just the same way Clarence Worthington first made them over 200 years ago. Our tradition of excellence dates back to the 1800s. This time-honored recipe is very old, okay? But who really cares? I mean, let's be honest. They're crackers. Either buy them or don't. But don't expect us to sit here and tell you some long story about the history of some freaking crackers. They're just crackers. Piss off."

A Picture (1,000 Words)

Four by six inches. Glossy. A lake. Me. Summer. I am on water skis behind a boat. I am holding on to a line as the boat pulls me. I am moving fast. I am wearing a red bathing suit and an orange life preserver. I am smiling. I am feeling happy and confident. I'm looking cool. And I am going really fast. Nice breeze. The wind is blowing through my hair. White water is spraying out behind me and off to the sides. I look awesome. This could be a postcard: the sunshine, the pine trees, the mountains, and me ripping it up on water skis in the middle of it all. I'm on a camping trip with a bunch of my friends. Some of them are in the boat. Others are watching from the dock. I can even feel the strangers on the beach watching me. Who's the man?! Right now that would be me. This is my moment.

I am happy this photo is being taken, because it is an official record of this moment. It's not like I'd forget a moment as cool as this, but it's nice to have an official document of it. Man, I cannot wait to see this photo. I am glad I chose to wear my sunglasses. They make me look even cooler. And to think I was reluctant to try waterskiing. Huh. Life sure is ironic sometimes. I didn't want to do it because I was afraid of falling, but then Janis, who just had a baby, tried it. After that, I would have been the only one who didn't do it, so I decided to go for it. I mean, I didn't want to be *that* guy. I'm happy my friends talked me into doing this. I'll have to thank Ed later. Definitely. This is going very well, especially as I'm trying to impress Julie, which I'd say is working right now. I bet I hook up with her tonight.

The great thing about meeting someone on a camping trip is that she doesn't have any preconceived notions about you. You get to present the best version of yourself, which is the one she wants to hook up with. And that version is the guy who was funny when we were pitching our tents and then was kind of aloof and mysterious when we were looking for firewood and is now cool and confident on water skis. I wisely didn't complain about my allergies or mention my fear of snakes at all. All of this is flashing through my head as I smile for the camera.

The look on my face says that I'm not worried about anything. Waterskiing is easier than I thought it would be. Why didn't I try this earlier? I'm posing for the camera. I'm waving with one hand. This is one of the coolest moments of my life, no question about that. I'm looking right into the lens of the camera, which is why I don't see the oncoming wake, where I probably should be looking.

This turns out to be the last moment just before I hit that wake.

Now that I look at myself I remember exactly what happened. A moment later my body spins completely out of control. I am struggling, desperately trying to maintain my balance. The boat swerves. Is Ed turning the boat? He is. Are you kidding me? Then everything starts to go into slow motion. I am wiping out. There is no saving it now. I am falling badly. The wipeout feels almost like it is punishing me for trying to avoid it. I go down. Face-first. My mouth is open—in fact, it couldn't be more open. I feel several hundred gallons of lake water go into my mouth. Water goes into my eyes, nose, ears, butt... every possible body hole. I continue to get dragged by the boat, because for some reason, I am still holding on to the line. Finally I let go. I am still moving forward, though. My water-logged body comes to a stop. I float there. I am disoriented. Angry. I knew this was a bad idea. Why did they make me do this? Then I discover that I am missing my bathing suit. Everyone is laughing. But I am not laughing. I am the only one not laughing.

Now I am trying to somehow still look cool. My sunglasses are gone. They left a nice cut in my forehead though. I'm searching for my bathing suit. When did it come off? Where the hell is it?! There it is. I grab it. I'm putting it back on in the lake. I'm getting out of the water.

Now I notice that my bathing suit is on backwards. Great. My so-called friends are laughing even more at me. These people suck. I am trying to be a good sport about this, but I am complaining. And I am blaming Ed. I yell at him and tell him he did this on purpose. That son of a bitch. I know it.

Ed just couldn't stand to see me actually getting the attention for once. I tell him this. Everyone stops laughing. Then I stop accusing him because I can see people are now looking at me like I'm the jerk.

I go shower off. And that's where I end up finding some things on my legs. Leeches!? Are you kidding me? Leeches! Nobody said anything about leeches in the lake. I am cursing as I pull leeches off my legs. That's when I see a snake. I run and scream. Julie is there, sitting with Ed. I hear her say to him, "He's just mad that he made an ass of himself and he's taking it out on you. What a creep. Don't worry about it, Ed." Ed and Julie hook up that night. I end up with a rash and some sort of sinus infection.

I'm going to rip up this picture now.

Epigrams, Fragments & Light Verse

The bird,
The bee,
The running child,
are all the same
to the sliding glass door.

———

Seek and ye shall find
or ye shall become frustrated
and start to bang things
and hurt thy hand
on the door of the kitchen cabinet.

———

Leave no stone unturned
In your quest to
disrupt a rock garden

———

Ask three economists the same question
And you will get four different answers
that are equally long and boring to
        listen to.

————

Man:
Never more like a snowstorm
than when he sneezes
whilst eating rice.

————

A typo can charge the meaning of anything.

————

In Physics:
Rate × Time = Distance

In Bed:
Rate × Time = Prostitute

————

The Pursuit of Happiness:
It sure seems to like a good chase, doesn't it?

————

Words have power,
you dumb piece of shit.

————

Let no man's deathbed
be a futon.

————

Worst of Both Worlds:
One example, the TV movie.

———

Every cloud has a silver lining.
Right. Okay.
And, tell me again how a silver lining helps me?

———

The best way to make somebody feel important is to try to assassinate them.

———

Spilling
floor cleaner
Only makes the
floor cleaner.

———

A scented candle left unwatched
soon becomes a larger scented candle,
whose scent is "entire house."

———

The lord works in mysterious ways.
Indeed.
And a shorter way to say that is:
God is a sneak.

———

The man who wins an argument with his barber,
    has won only the verbal portion of the argument.

———

What a cruel, ironic, little joke
Nature has played on man
By making the dumbest people the loudest ones
I'm talking to you, sports fan.

———

This is not my best epigram.

———

A Wish Granted:
If only I could be sold more things, more of the time by larger and larger corporations.

———

Relationships,
like eyebrows,
are better when there is
a space between them.

———

Nothing wise
Was ever printed
Upon an apron

———

THE MEDIA: more content = more discontent.

———

A Question of Degree:
Is the man with
the beard of bees really any more
impressive than the one with
the mustache of bees?

———

On Fleeting Youth:
One moment,
an escape artist,
The next,
a man who needs help getting out of a chair.

———

I wish
This poem
Were longer.

There,
That's better.

———

If these walls could talk,
what secrets they would share,
and how muffled those secrets would be
by all the wallpaper there.

———

What is a fairy tale, but a lie with a nice ending.

———

"It is better to kill someone with kindness."
Indeed, it is.
May I suggest showering them with gifts, very heavy gifts.

———

The Liar and the Truth Teller:
I came to a fork in the road
where there was a liar and a truth teller
Luckily, I had a gun
So both quickly became truth tellers.

I was a tree hugger
once
during a storm.

———

Never be less interesting than your refrigerator magnets.

———

Our Times, a Brief History:
As televisions became flatter,
People became rounder.

———

One Phone Call

—Hello.

—Hello? Jeff. Oh, thank God! It's me, Allen.

—Hey.

—Listen, man, I need your help. I'm in prison and—

—Can you speak up? I can barely hear you.

—*(louder)* It's Allen. I'm in prison. There's been some sort of mix-up and I've been arrested. They think I committed a murder! But I haven't done anything. It's a long story. Listen, I *really* need your help. I've only got this one phone call, and they're about to transfer me to another prison—

—Okay.

—I don't have my ID or anything on me. I left it all on my desk by mistake. I need you to go to my place and grab my ID and my pills. Please don't forget the pills—that's the medicine I need to take every—

—I think there's something wrong with the connection. I still can't really hear you.

—It's probably the payphone I'm using in the prison. Did you hear any of what I was saying? I'm in major trouble and I don't have much time. They're going to extradite me to Cuba, because they think I'm—

—I'm just messing with you. I'm actually not here. This is Jeff's voicemail. Gotcha! *(laughs)* I'm in Europe until late August. Leave me a message after the beep. Laters. *(beep)* This user's mailbox is full and unable to accept any messages at this time.

More Drawings

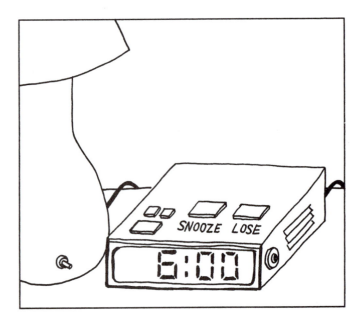

Snowglobe with frustrated man trying to shovel driveway.

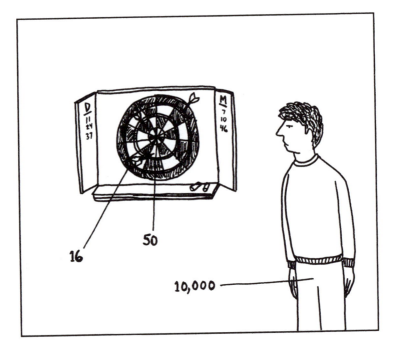

IMPORTANT

VERY
IMPORTANT

Dog-with-rash Lampshade.

Superhero flying through flock
(just to be a dick).

Come on, Pie!

Dead Gravestone Dealer.

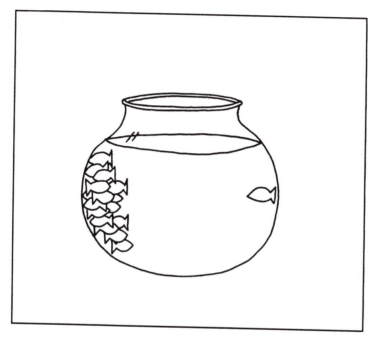

Fish Fart.

FOUR

My Powers

Before you even think of coming near me, I should warn you that I have powers, and not just ordinary powers. I have super powers. I may appear to be average, but I can assure you I am anything but.

For starters, I can see the future, both during and after it's happened.

I can also hold my breath for hours at a time in my hands. And speaking of my hands...they are lethal weapons. They are so lethal that I often keep them tied to my sides lest I accidentally kill myself with them.

I can leap over the edge of tall buildings in a single bound, and I sometimes imagine doing it when I feel kind of depressed. But even though I know I can, I don't, five times so far.

One of my greatest strengths is strength. I can crush an ice cream cone on my forehead like it's a soda can, and then I can patiently wait for the ice cream to drip down into the lickable area of my face, and never even get a napkin.

In a fire, I am extra flammable, which I am likely to use to my advantage.

I can speed-read, especially anything printed on a T-shirt with large breasts beneath it.

I am a keen observer of human behavior, often from a perch or from behind some bushes. And when it comes to emotions, I can switch from crying to laughing in a matter of weeks.

I can shoot lasers out of my fingers, though I prefer not to because it requires a lot of set-up time.

And I can keep a secret better than...don't you wish you knew.

When it's very windy, I don't complain. And when there is also rain mixed with the wind, I complain very little. But, if I'm in a bad mood, you'll know it, because I can sulk so powerfully that it makes everyone who is anywhere near me kind of annoyed.

I am a fierce competitor. During board games, I destroy my enemies completely or argue with them until they don't want to play anymore.

If you come at me in the wild, be warned. You will be outmatched. I have been known to communicate with animals who have twice my intelligence and then really agitate them.

I can make any doctor go crazy, just by asking him a series of basically identical questions, each with slightly different wording, about the thing on my back.

Dentists fear me, because while they are focusing on my teeth, I am focusing on their crotch.

I can kill someone's cat with a yo-yo, and probably on purpose too.

I am versatile. I can work with or without a sidekick. I can even work against a sidekick. Villains fear me because I am unpredictable and broccoli. See what I mean?

My weaknesses are few. I am sometimes too strong, like when I'm hugging a loud child or shaking the hand of an ex-girlfriend's new boyfriend. I have been told that I don't know my own strength by more than one arts and crafts teacher. My only real weakness is lava—and that's only *before* it cools. Also, I have some severe food allergies.

I am helpful and I am honest. If I see an old lady trying to cross a street, I will tell her she is old. I very rarely steal anything. And if I do, it's only because I know I could probably find a use for it eventually.

I can run fast. How fast? Why don't you ask again, and raise your voice this time, because now I'm way over here.

My vision is impeccable. I can see through the clothes of anyone who is wearing something white who I've just sprayed with water.

I have a strong sense of justice, especially when someone tries to cut in front of me in line or break up with me.

When it comes to hearing, mine is legendary. I can become self-conscious about what two people are saying about me from the other side of a party. And when I can't hear, I read their lips or go over and ask them what they were saying.

I am immune to poison, unless I ingest it; but even then, I put up a pretty impressive fight.

Also, my swimming has been described as "very disturbing."

And if we're eating potato chips, good luck keeping up with me.

Finally, I am a bleeder. So, if you still think you want to fight me, why don't you consider the mess you're going to make.

That's what I thought.

Human Cannonball
Occupational Hazards

Getting into the cannon after somebody has left a cannonball in there and then getting shot point-blank with the cannonball and falling out of the front of the cannon.

Getting shot *into* the cannon (due to backfire).

Loss of hearing and/or entire body.

Inability to enjoy movies about pirates or old sea battles.

Getting shot out of the cannon and then colliding, in mid air, with another human cannonball who was shot out of a nearby cannon.

Recurring, being-shot-out-of-a-cannon night terrors.

After climbing into cannon, helmet gets stuck in the shaft of cannon. The cannon fires and shoots entire body into helmet.

The cannon won't fire; while looking inside to see what is wrong with it, the cannon fires and shoots head off of body.

Ennui.

Eulogy

Rod. What can you say about Rod? He was one of a kind. He was so full of life. And even though he didn't have a very long life, he totally squeezed everything he could out of the time he had. I mean, just think about how many times he stayed out all night clubbing.

Rod was one of my best friends. He was one of my "boys." He was my "homie," my "dawg," my "nigga"...not literally, of course, because he was white, like me. We used to call each other that just as a joke. And, man, it was funny every time.

Rod might have been white but he had a heart of gold, both in the sense of being a good guy and in the sense that he had that big gold heart that he used to wear with his other bling whenever he went out. Man, Rod had some great gold chains. If you saw him out at a club or fighting somebody in a parking lot, you'd think he was a millionaire or a rapper, or both. That was Rod. That was how he rolled. You know, Rod was the first guy I ever heard use the term "roll" that way. He'd say "Let's roll" or "Time to roll, bitches" or just "Roll!" What a badass.

And, damn, he sure was good with words. Rod was so quick. It always amazed me how he could come up with shit off the top of his head, like nicknames. He'd meet someone and within like

20 seconds he'd have a whole nickname for them. "Okay, blue shirt," he'd say or "Slow down, big ears." I remember the night he banged that girl on the stairs at Temptations. He had just met her and he was already calling her "Dollface." And you know what? She looked exactly like a doll when it came to her face. He was perceptive like that.

On top of being smart, Rod also had great style. He always looked like a player, especially when he rolled. All I need to say is "wifebeater and fedora" and anyone who knew Rod knows exactly what I'm talking about.

Even though he was cool, Rod never forgot where he came from. Probably because he never actually left where he came from. Sure, Rod used to talk about moving out of his parents' house someday, but he also talked about just chillin' there to see if he could eventually inherit it or something. Rod was a patient guy.

When I was asked to give Rod's eulogy, so many memories started to go through my head: working out at the gym with Rod, drinking, tanning, playing video games, the time we double-teamed that drunk chick in the hotel Jacuzzi. Rod was a true friend. If you needed advice or a condom, he would give it to you, no questions asked. And he always had great sunglasses. Of course, he would never let you touch them, but you couldn't blame him. They were really expensive and they looked awesome on him.

"Bros before hos." That's what Rod used to say. He was loyal to his friends. But, at the same time, if he really wanted to nail a girl, he would find a way to make it happen, even if it meant taking her from one of his friends. That might sound weird or like a para-dox or something. I guess it was. That was part of what made Rod interesting. He was unpredictable and mysterious. Ladies loved it. I can tell you that for a fact. Rod was a legend when it came to get-ting ladies to meet "Rod's rod" as he called it.

Rod was such a funny guy. He was always quick with a joke or a punch to your nuts if you weren't looking or if you dozed off or something. And if there happened to be someone around who had a weakness or some kind of an insecurity, Rod knew just how to focus right in on it and turn it into a good joke, especially if there was a bunch of us there to egg him on. And if that person got upset about it, Rod would just keep going at it until they learned to lighten up. That's the kind of guy Rod was. He'd make you laugh but he'd also make you think. You'd think, "I hope he doesn't do that to me." And you always knew that if you turned it around on him he'd kick your ass. He was a true leader.

People always noticed Rod. Whether it was his cologne or the bass booming from his Hummer. Rod was the kind of guy you just could not ignore. He used to crank that thing up so loud that people in other cars would look over and shake their heads like "Man, I wish I had a system like that."

A lot of people don't know this, but Rod really knew how to have fun with a sunroof, probably better than anyone I ever knew. He would stand up in the open sunroof of a limo and scream out of it for blocks and blocks. He didn't care. He made people on Spring break look like pussies. Rod was on permanent Spring break. For real. I mean, sometimes he would drink so much that he would just start punching anybody who came near him.

Rod also had a creative side. One look at his hair told you that. And if you tried to touch it, good luck with your broken fingers.

Rod would light up a room whenever he walked into it, literally, with a flashlight, when he was working as a bouncer. He used to shine that light onto girls' butts or right at their tits. He made everyone feel like a star. Rod was the kind of guy you wanted to be like, because he was no nonsense. I remember one time when he wouldn't let some little geek into the club after the geek kept saying "But my fiancée's in there!" Rod finally belted the guy and shut him up right then and there. The policy was no geeky guys allowed in, period, and Rod honored it, because he was a professional. He was really dedicated to his job. Sometimes there would be a fight going on and Rod would just join in and pummel whoever looked weaker. And I mean *pummel*. Talk about professional.

Rod had a lot of honor. If someone bumped into his shoulder in a club or gave him attitude, he would not put up with that shit. You didn't mess with his honor, because if you did you got a beatdown. Plain and simple. There aren't a lot of people who stick to their principles like that nowadays. A lot of them pussy out or want to try to talk their way out of a situation. Not Rod. He was always man enough to let his fists do the talking. And they talked to anyone who needed to listen, including chicks who thought they could get away with their bullshit.

Nobody got off easy if they were messing with Rod's honor, not even family. I remember when Rod's brother accused him of taking money from their grandparents' savings, Rod pounded him so bad he had to go to the hospital. "There's a difference between 'taking' and 'borrowing'" he said. Rod fully intended to pay back some of that money eventually. I know that for a fact, because he mentioned it so many times over the years.

I think what I'll miss most about Rod is how awesome it was to go clubbing with him.

I'm sad Rod is gone, but I feel happy knowing that he died doing something he loved: an underage girl.

Flags

Flags have been an important part of our world for centuries. Unfortunately many of them are outdated. I have included here a few suggestions for updating some of these old flags. I have also provided some ideas for new flags.

Flag for the South
This flag features a man wearing a nice suit, holding a Bible and a waffle. He looks proud and is standing inside a trailer park.

The Olympic Flag
A white flag that has the words "Nice try, Finland" printed across the middle of it.

The City of Boston
This flag features a picture of a drunk guy who wants to fight you. The more the wind flaps the flag, the more drunk the guy looks, and the more he wants to fight you. Also, he has a crew cut and looks sort of Irish.

Flag Representing Blind People
Anything goes with this one. The important thing is that the design is not that offensive.

The Army
A man in a uniform, who is shaking your hand, but it's no longer attached to your body.

Harvard University
A picture of a person who went to Harvard. Under the picture there is an inscription of a Latin phrase: *Vestri alma materia ut exsisto memoratus quam primum in sermo.* The translation: "Your alma mater: to be mentioned as soon as possible in conversation."

New Jersey
A picture of the rest of the country feeling embarrassed.

McDonald's
A cow wearing sunglasses. He is holding a hamburger and smoking a cigarette while giving a thumb's-up. In the background there is some sort of propeller or chopping machine coming towards him.

Flag for Responding to an Enemy Who Is Trying to Surrender
This flag could be useful during battle when one side waves a white flag to surrender, but the other side wants to keep fighting. This flag is white but it also has a middle finger made out of blood in the center of it. When you wave this flag you're responding to the surrender by saying, "Tough shit."

Mexico
A drawing of Mexico with arrows pointing out of it.

THE ANDERSON FAMILY (FROM MY OLD NEIGHBORHOOD)
The whole family is on the flag. The dad is kind of drunk, as usual. The mom has that WASPy angry-mixed-with-uppity look on her face. The daughter looks cute and seems like she'd be a good girlfriend but turns out to be a cheater. She's acting like she loves you, but she just clearly made out with one of your friends. Off to the side we see their dog, who so easily blends in with the pavement that he could very easily be innocently run over by anyone.

Painted Faces

People Who Paint
Their Faces

1. Warriors
2. Clowns
3. Diehard Football Fans
4. Drag Queens

People Who
Lack Subtlety

1. Warriors
2. Clowns
3. Diehard Football Fans
4. Drag Queens

People Who I Do Not Want to Be Around

1. Warriors
2. Clowns
3. Diehard Football Fans
4. Drag Queens

People Who Are Probably Not Reading This

1. Warriors
2. Clowns
3. Diehard Football Fans
4. Drag Queens

Some Meanings

z z z z z z z z z z z z   a person sleeping

b z z z z z z z z z z z   a bee flying

z z z z z z b z z z z z   a bee that is sleeping and then wakes up and starts flying

b z z z z z t   a bee that is getting killed by a person who was sleeping but then woke up

———

af;kjnabakjoiwenpt   a cat walking on a keyboard

iamwhiskersbeware   a smart cat walking on a keyboard

———

n   a half-eaten M&M

m   two half-eaten M&M's carefully placed together

##%@&%*#$!&	cursing
########%@&%	cursing, with a stutter

———

haha	a person laughing
muahahahaha	a villain laughing
ha	a person starting to sneeze
muaha	a villain starting to sneeze
ahamuahahaha	a villain discovering a person who is starting to sneeze; and then laughing

———

xoxoxoxo	kisses and hugs
oxoxoxox	oxen
xxxxxxxx	a very dirty movie
oooooooo	a sound heard during a very dirty movie
oooxoxox	a sound heard during a very dirty movie in which someone kisses and hugs oxen

———

(((((((((	nail clippings (of an anal-retentive man)

I	self
i	self as baby
i i i i i i i i i ii i i i i	self as baby in nursery (with set of Siamese twins in there, too)
———	
U U	prints made by a horse standing on its hind legs
U o	prints made by a horse that has a wooden leg standing on its hind legs
o o	prints made by a horse with two wooden legs (impressive)
———	
.	an atom (close up)
.	a galaxy (far away)
.	an atom, close up, in a galaxy far away
———	
T	the beginning of THE END
D	the end of THE END

Goreburg and Spatz

Arthur Goreburg arrived at Zell Laboratories three days after graduating from MIT. He had fielded offers from every major lab and think tank in the country. There was even an offer from a small but prestigious concentrate tank in Sweden. For Arthur, though, there was never any doubt that he would end up at Zell.

Zell Labs had been the nation's leading research and technology lab for more than half a century, producing nine Nobel Laureates, countless technological breakthroughs, and very little sex. Its hallways teemed with many of the world's greatest minds, many of them bona fide geniuses, and even more of them social disasters. Goreburg would be Zell's new wonderboy. And with his formidable brain, pimpled face, and catastrophic sense of style, Arthur fit the part perfectly.

Until Arthur's arrival, Zell's reigning wonderboy was Ronald Spatz. Now two years into his employ at Zell, Spatz had earned a reputation for calculating large sums in his head at lightning speed. He was also one of Zell's biggest showoffs (he once solved a Rubik's Cube using only his butt cheeks). Like many of his colleagues, Ronald was a know-it-all. And he had a notoriously small bladder. Still, Ronald was a great dancer and could be a lot of fun at a party, if he'd ever gone to one.

Goreburg and Spatz did not speak much to each other during Goreburg's first few months at Zell. In the lab's stratified, cloistered ecosystem of elite thinkers, the two young scientists were natural enemies. Each was eager to prove himself, and neither wanted the other to do so first.

Spatz was already getting tired of hearing about the "new kid" Goreburg, and Goreburg, for his part, thought Spatz had a particularly punchable-looking face. So, the two young bucks tactfully avoided each other and managed to keep a cordial distance.

Then one afternoon, just after the company's annual laser picnic, where for the first time in years no one got burned or blinded, the director of commercial engineering, Bill Dingle, called the two young scientists into his office.

"I need you two to work on something very important for us," said Dingle in his patented monotone voice (it had been patented earlier that year for use in an autistic robot).

Goreburg and Spatz listened, both trying not to appear too excited about the opportunity.

Dingle continued. "It's a copy machine."

The two men slouched with disappointment, their already muscle-less frames looking even more flaccid than usual. "A copy machine?" thought Goreburg. "What a joke."

Spatz let out a contemptuous sigh.

Sensing their disappointment, Bill quickly explained the assignment. "I am not talking about a conventional copy machine. I'm talking about something much more advanced, a new kind of copy machine. We need to create a machine that can copy something but make the copy look like it's a completely different idea from the original. So that way the copy appears to be the result of 'parallel thought' or just some sort of an innocent coincidence."

Arthur and Ronald listened. Both men now seemed interested.

"People in Hollywood have expressed strong interest in such a device, especially the large movie studios," Dingle explained.

Goreburg started brainstorming immediately, his beady eyes dart-ing back and forth behind his glasses. Spatz, equally intrigued by the task, started to rock with excitement, and also because he had to pee.

Dingle explained that two major advertising agencies had already offered millions for a working model. He and his partners knew that that kind of machine would be virtually priceless to the advertising industry, an industry that had been built on stealing other people's ideas and then changing them slightly to make shitty commercials out of them.

The two rivals left Dingle's office. They began working together the next morning.

If Goreburg and Spatz could figure out how to make this new kind of copy machine, it would mean huge profits for Zell, and more importantly, major recognition for the two young scientists.

From the very start, Goreburg and Spatz hated working together. They were competitive and distant. Arthur was a slob, which irked the legendarily anal-retentive Spatz. And Ronald irritated Arthur with his weird tapping habit. But, the more they worked together, the more they discovered just how much they had in common. For one thing, both were allergic to legumes. Also, as children, both had been rolled down a hill inside a tire by neighborhood bullies, which was for both of them a memorable first lesson in physics. Finally, and, perhaps most importantly, both spent a lot of time alone making things in their basements.

Spatz had developed several minor inventions, most notable among them a tiny nuclear bomb that could be used to kill a frog or a very old person. He hoped to market it overseas, perhaps to some of the smaller nations who had smaller enemies. He had also done pioneering research in the field of historical biochemistry, recreating chemical models of famous historical figures' breath based on their diets and ethnic origins.

Goreburg, in his basement, had designed several specialty vehicles, including a hovercraft 'made from a vacuum cleaner' and a vacuum cleaner 'made from a hovercraft.'

After work they started to hang out and talk about their favorite movies and about the woman who worked at Zell. Their opinions about both were based firmly in science fiction. Before long, Arthur and Ronald were collaborating outside of work. One night, while they were hovering in Arthur's vacuum cleaner, they started to talk about time travel.

They both knew that there had been various attempts to build time machines at the lab before. No one had succeeded. A few years earlier it looked like one scientist came close—he had managed to jump into the future by a couple of minutes, but later it turned out that he had just passed out in his machine. Another scientist managed to send himself backwards through time but only metabolically—he sent his body back to puberty, which had terrible repercussions on his marriage.

They knew that a time machine presented difficult questions: "If time travel were possible, wouldn't it have always been possible?" and "Isn't there a paradox in existing in a time before you existed?" and "How could you eat something twice?" They agreed to leave these questions aside and let their work lead them wherever it led them.

Working late every night after work, they tried various things. One step forward, two steps back, and then one to the right.

Finally, they had a breakthrough. Using a collection of old watches, a network of satellite servers, and some uranium, they managed to make a small machine. What they needed in order to make the machine work was a tear in the time-space continuum. Luckily, Goreburg had discovered one just above the liquor store on the edge of town. If his calculations were correct, then the machine could pass through the tear and enable them to travel backwards through time.

They put the finishing touches on the machine and decided

to launch it after work that Friday. They rented a moving truck, loaded the time machine inside it, and drove to the liquor store, where they parked next to the wormhole. Just after the night clerk closed the liquor store and drove away, they wheeled out the time machine. Over dinner they had agreed to make the first trip something that would create good press and age well for posterity. So, they strapped themselves in and set out for July 4, 1776, to see the signing of the Declaration of Independence.

There was a whir and a boom. The machine filled with smoke and everything got blurry. There were some flashes of light and then a kaleidoscope of colors. A moment later, everything stopped and the machine was silent. Both men were dazed, but perfectly fine. The smoke started to clear and Spatz unbuckled his seatbelt. He got up and looked out the window. "I think it worked!" he shouted.

Goreburg was stunned. He had never been so happy in his life. He unhinged his seatbelt and ran to the window. Outside, people in Colonial attire walked around. Some cautiously approached the machine. This was real. They had done it.

Arthur turned the doorknob and pushed the door. Nothing happened. He pushed harder. The door would not open. "It's jammed," he said. Ronald looked at him. "What do you mean?"

"I mean the door won't open."

"Let me check the external camera," Spatz said as he walked over to a small console. He typed into a keyboard and looked at the screen.

"Uh-oh," he said quietly.

"What?" responded Goreburg, still trying to open the door.

Spatz called him over. "Take a look at this," he said.

Goreburg looked at the screen. He could not believe his eyes. They had landed perfectly between two trees. The machine was wedged between the trees, and the door was jammed right against one of them. There was no way out of it. As they sat there, just a few hundred yards away, the founding fathers were signing the Declaration of Independence.

"Shit," said Goreburg. "Can't you do something about this?"

"Me?" replied Spatz. "I thought you were supposed to be the genius, Arthur."

"Shut up, Ronald," Goreburg snapped.

By now, a small group of Philadelphians were gathered around the time machine. Ronald and Arthur had landed just behind a pub, which attracted quite a crowd. Now several drunk and rowdy colonists were starting to rock the machine back and forth.

"Let's get the hell out of here," said Ronald.

Arthur agreed. They strapped themselves in and headed for their second choice, AD 33, the crucifixion of Jesus Christ. The machine started to spark and whir, and a moment later they were off again. When the smoke cleared they found themselves in Jersualem in the year AD 33. Again, amazingly, the machine had worked. They congratulated each other. A moment later Ronald popped out of his seat and ran to the door. He pushed it. It didn't budge. He pushed harder. Again, no luck.

This time when they looked at the external camera they found themselves jammed against the wall of a cave.

"You've got to be kidding me," complained Goreburg. "What the hell is going on?"

"It's a time machine, Arthur. Shit happens," snarled Spatz.

"Yeah, well, that's the problem, isn't it? We've got a time machine, but what we need is a time *and space* machine, Mr. Wizard," said Goreburg.

"Maybe you've forgotten that time and space are linked in a little something called 'spacetime,' Ronald. I thought someone with your intelligence would know that."

"Shut up, Arthur."

"You shut up!" Then both men realized that if they didn't stop arguing and head back to the present quickly, their energy source would run out. They stopped talking, put on their seatbelts, and headed home. The next day, the two men returned to work and exchanged awkward apologies. Goreburg promised to work on providing a longer-lasting energy source, and Spatz offered to solve the space problem. As frustrated as both of them were, they were also elated. Each realized just how monumental their invention was. And both secretly wished he could cut the other guy out of it. But both men also knew that they needed each other, at least for the time being. So they kept quiet and worked to improve the machine.

A week later, Spatz had solved the space problem. And the next day Goreburg delivered a new energy source and they were ready to go.

Spatz suggested that they head to ancient Egypt to witness the completion of the Pyramids.

They went back to the liquor store and headed to Egypt. When they landed right on the tip of the Great Pyramid, Spatz looked at Goreburg.

"You happy?" he said. "I fixed the space problem; we've landed exactly on the tip of the Pyramid. You're welcome."

Goreburg, enraged by Spatz's stunt, got out of his seat to punch him.

"No!" cried Spatz. "You'll throw off our balance."

The machine tipped and started to roll down the side of the Great Pyramid.

Spatz scrambled, reached for the controls, and quickly typed in anything he could. The machine activated, and a moment later they were gone.

They landed in a random field somewhere in an isolated part of Eastern Europe in the year 1356. Goreburg opened the door and looked out of the machine. There was nothing there aside from some shrubs and a few small animals.

Goreburg looked at Spatz and, in his most sarcastic tone, said, "Nice one, Ronald."

"Shut up, Arthur," Spatz replied as he marched through the door of the time machine. The trip was too much for his tiny bladder. He was desperate to relieve himself, and was just happy that he could finally pee. He walked outside and headed for some taller shrubs off in the distance.

As he peed, Ronald surveyed the landscape before him. While there were no people or any signs of culture there, it was still thrilling to be standing in a field in 1356, peeing on a medieval shrub. He started to think about what they'd accomplished. Then, suddenly a loud noise interrupted Spatz's reverie. He turned to see the time machine power up and recede into a cloud of smoke.

Inside the machine, Goreburg sat in his seat and smiled to himself as he headed off with the machine to claim the massive fame and fortune that awaited him in the future. Arthur looked through the window and smirked at the sight of a panic-stricken Spatz sprinting towards the machine with his pants falling around his legs.

Then, in an instant, Goreburg and the machine were gone.

Spatz screamed and collapsed.

Goreburg settled into his seat, overcome with joy and relief. He'd never have to see Spatz again. He was eager to get home and make plans to market the time machine. "I'm going to be a very rich man," he said to himself.

Then the machine made a weird clicking sound and began to spin around. The noise faded and the machine started to shut down. It coasted for a moment and then crashed into the ground.

The machine had been damaged when it tumbled down the side of the Great Pyramid. In his haste to abandon Ronald, Arthur failed to notice the damage. Now, after using it in its damaged condition, the machine was completely destroyed. Goreburg looked at the date on the console. He had only traveled about one week into the future and only about two hundred yards from where he left Spatz.

A week later Spatz showed up, and when he found Arthur standing near the broken machine, he beat the hell out of him.

Spatz would have killed Goreburg had the fight not been broken up by a group of local tribesmen. The tribesmen had seen the
crash from a distance and hiked up to the field to investigate it.

They seized Arthur and Ronald and brought them back to their
village.

A week later Goreburg and Spatz were tried for witchcraft and
burned at the stake. No one ever knew what happened to the
young scientists. Even though they vanished, their copy machine
did not. It was successfully tested and then sold to Hollywood,
where it is still widely used today.

Confessions of a White Guy with Dreadlocks

Even though I play it down, I secretly love the attention that my dreadlocks get me.

I often go to events where I know I can shake my head around a lot and showcase my dreadlocks. This includes concerts, drum circles, and tennis matches.

If I go somewhere and there is another white guy with dreadlocks there, I get competitive. I prefer to be the only white guy with dreadlocks in the group, because the dreadlocks are kind of my thing.

I honestly can't tell you when the last time I washed my hair was. In fact, I don't even remember what season it was.

I think white guys with cornrows look ridiculous.

I didn't actually come up with my personal tag line: "Don't dread the locks." I heard some other guy with dreadlocks say it at Burning Man.

I own more hacky sacks than books.

I always try to keep a safe distance from cats and squirrels, because if I get too close they'll crawl onto my head and try to burrow into my dreadlocks.

My parents pay my rent.

One time, when I was lying down in a park I accidentally got a whiff of my dreadlocks, and I almost passed out from the smell.

I secretly hate the sound of bongos. The main reason I play them is because they go really well with my look (and they're a great excuse for me to shake my dreads around).

I do not actually know how to play the bongos.

Fireworks make me very uneasy, because if one of them flies into my hair, my dreads will light up like flash paper.

If someone tries to out-mellow me, I'll put my dreadlocks into overdrive, making it clear who the mellow one is here.

I am not as smart as I look.

Spanish Teacher

The following is a translation of a conversation that took place entirely in Spanish.

SPANISH TEACHER: Thomas?

FORMER STUDENT: *(stopping)* Señora Alvarez? Hi.

SPANISH TEACHER: Thomas, hello, it's great to see you! How have you been?

FORMER STUDENT: Good.

SPANISH TEACHER: It's been a long time since high school. What have you been up to?

FORMER STUDENT: Yes. It has many years of . . . that . . . when high school. Good. How you?

SPANISH TEACHER: I see you still remember some of your Spanish. Very good . . . Well, as for me, I'm doing well. I had another little girl. Wait, now that I think about it, I wasn't even married yet when you took my class. Well, anyway I'm happily married, and I have two little girls now. Of course, I'm still teaching Spanish.

FORMER STUDENT: Good. Yes. Good. I work. I live. I am . . . I am a . . . do work. And there is money. When with . . . ? Yes. Good.

SPANISH TEACHER: Okay. So you have no idea what I'm saying, do you? I'm guessing that no matter what I say you'll just say "Good" back to me. Is that right?

FORMER STUDENT: Good.

SPANISH TEACHER: Yep. Well that's great. Another former student who retained nothing. Thomas, if you're a complete moron, say "Good."

FORMER STUDENT: Good.

SPANISH TEACHER: Shocker. Students like you make me want to cut my own tongue out.

FORMER STUDENT: Yes. Good. I...table, go much...tapas good.

SPANISH TEACHER: Wow. You're even dumber than I remember, and yet it's amazing that you insist on sticking with the Spanish here. And now I'll make it sound like I'm asking you a question?

FORMER STUDENT: Yes. Yes. Good. Um...

SPANISH TEACHER: I remember when you were in high school how you had a crush on me. It was fun to tease you in those subtle little ways. I bet you still fantasize about me. I have to say, if I weren't married I'd take you back to my place right now and have some fun with you.

FORMER STUDENT: I have went college and...avocado.

SPANISH TEACHER: "Avocado." Do you mean "lawyer"? Are you trying to say "lawyer"?

FORMER STUDENT: No. Me not avocado.

SPANISH TEACHER: You mean you're not a "lawyer"? Is that what you mean? The word is "l-a-w-y-e-r."

FORMER STUDENT: A-v-o-c-a-d-o.

SPANISH TEACHER: Whatever...So you're not a lawyer. Why are you telling me this?

FORMER STUDENT: Uh, how say..."paralegal"?

SPANISH TEACHER: Oh, you could use the word "underachiever" or "disappointment."

FORMER STUDENT: Yes. "Disappointment," yes. Me that.

SPANISH TEACHER: Good. Very good.

FORMER STUDENT: Yes. Me not avocado. The much with good. Yes. much...um...papers?

SPANISH TEACHER: You know what, if I were single I would get weird with you. If I could just find a way to stop you from talking...maybe put a cloth in your mouth or something. I wonder who this girl is who seems to be with you? Is this your girlfriend? I doubt it. I'd think you could do better than her.

FORMER STUDENT: Oh, yes! It me forget...um...This is girl-friend, Inez. She from Spain.

SPANISH TEACHER: ...

INEZ: Hello. Pleased to make your acquaintance.

SPANISH TEACHER:...

Zing!

Information Booth

GUY WORKING IN BOOTH: Can I help you?

ME: Yes. I'm trying to find someone who is a disappointment to his parents.

Zing!

Airplane

WOMAN SITTING NEXT TO ME ON AIRPLANE: So, what do you do?

ME: Oh, I get paid to make boring small talk with strangers on airplanes.

Zing!
—And then sat in hostile silence for next 5 hours of flight.

City Street

WOMAN: Do you know what time it is?

ME: Yeah. Let me see. *(looking at watch)* It looks like just past dumb question from annoying woman.

Zing!

My Friend's Apartment

MY FRIEND: I don't ever get to travel.

ME: Yeah, except for around the sun, every day, all the time.

Zing!

Coffee Shop

ME: *(paying at register, looking at jar that says "Tips" and then knocking it over)* Yeah, I guess it does.

Zing!

Club

GUY WHO HANGS OUT A LOT IN CLUBS: How does my hair look?

ME: It looks embarrassed.

Zing!
—Then got punched in the face.

Concert Hall

FULL ORCHESTRA: *(finishes playing long symphony)*

ME: *(before anyone can make a sound)* Nice try.

Zing!
—Then was lunged at by furious conductor.

Mirror

MY REFLECTION: What are you looking at?

ME: I don't know, a two-dimensional jackass?

Zing!
—And zinged at the same time.

Hospital

SURGEON: We're going to put you under now. Any questions before your surgery begins?

ME: Just one. Is that your breath or did a small animal die really close to your mouth?

Zing!
—Then immediately regretted it based on look on surgeon's face.[1]

---

[1] NOTE: This turned out to be the final Zing.

Results of Your Personality Test

Summary Report

Your Personal Career Profile Assessment outlines your skills, abilities, interests, strengths, weaknesses, personality characteristics, and suggested career matches for your type.

You will find your Profile and Results below.

Your Test Results

Your personality is suspicious, noncompliant, introverted, sneaky, untrustworthy, vengeful, greedy, unreasonable, and dangerous. You are naturally uncooperative and do not work well with others, at all. You are not a leader. Nor are you a follower. You are a disruptor. In addition, you are snarky, mean, pessimistic, and extremely unpleasant to be around. You are also very focused, but mostly on yourself. You are best suited for work that does not involve other people, that is, if you had any capacity for work whatsoever, which you don't.

You are cranky, immature, insensitive, and extremely unforgiving. Considering these characteristics, aim for careers that relate to your top interests and compliment you as a person.

Listed below are strengths that are typical of people who score like you. Consider occupations that will enable you to capitalize on these strengths.

Personality Strengths
- Judgmental
- Opportunistic
- Stubborn
- Slothful, self-indulgent, and self-pitying
- Prone to complaining
- Unsympathetic to others
- Extremely complacent
- May take unnecessary risks that put others in danger
- May have an attitude of superiority
- Tendency to inexplicably punch things

Shown below are non-strengths that are typical of people who score like you. These are areas where improvement will benefit your performance. It is best to minimize exposure in areas that might showcase your non-strengths.

Personality Non-strengths
- Tendency to kick or shove people when confused
- Easily confused
- Overly sensitive
- Propensity for blindly following dogmas
- Formidably lethargic
- Morally bankrupt
- Quick to start stabbing things when agitated
- Prone to uncontrollable weeping

- Uncomfortable in group social activities; can appear un-friendly and/or homicidal

Your extremely high score on the DOMINANCE scale indicates that you are naturally motivated to have absolute control over your environment and over anyone in it.

Your very low-range score on the CONSCIENTIOUSNESS scale suggests that you have the ability to be both precise and ruthless. You should be careful around babies and law-enforcement officials.

Some Possible Careers

Drug mule
Bouncer
Reality TV personality
Exterminator
Network television executive
Human shield
Civil War reenactor
DMV employee
Dental hygienist

Conclusion

This Career Assessment Profile has included a lot of helpful information, which you should take some time to process. If you do your best to apply your strengths and address your non-strengths you will fulfill your career and personality potential. Also, given your particular profile, it is important that you try your hardest not to kill anyone.

More Statistics

Every year drunk driving is responsible for over 20,000 stories that start with "Bro…"

"Yes" actually means "No" 100% of the time, when the question is "Can I give you some advice?"

For the price of just one cup of coffee you can feed a child a coffee.

4 in every 8 math teachers think that they should be 1 in every 2 math teachers.

Europe contains more than 85% of the world's armpit hair.

The leading killer of daredevils is the ground.

The chances that this statistic makes sense are 1.2% in 5/9 out of π.

In a blind taste test, 100% of the people tested preferred the taste of things that were not just shoved into their mouth by surprise without any warning.

Surveys indicate that 1 in every 1 person is you.

Over 370 trillion points are earned in pinball every year, which totals less than 1 impressive achievement per year.

If every person took 5 minutes less time in the shower, then people who take showers that are only 5 minutes long would start to smell.

Anvils appear 1000% more frequently in cartoons than in real life.

The average American household contains 2.5 television sets and 4.5 idiots.

1 in every 20 people is double-jointed. The other 19 really don't care or need to see a demonstration.

It is safer to fly in a plane than it is to fly in a car.

Excerpts from My Often-True Autobiography

"I love you," she whispered into my ear. I was quiet for a moment. Then I turned to her and said, "I love you too, darling," but I kind of burped it. It was all in one long burp. I could have done more words with it too, but I decided to cut it short. I remember the look in her eyes. It wasn't a good look.

There's an old Russian saying that goes some way or another. I don't know it. And I don't speak Russian. But I sometimes think about it and wonder if it is relevant to what I am going through at the time. But, probably not. I mean, what do Russians know about hunger, anyway?

As soon as I jumped out of the airplane, I realized I had forgotten my parachute. Thank God we were still on the runway.

When people said, "Why does your grandma have a mustache?"

we'd say, "Because she's Italian." And when they said, "And why the top hat?" we started to realize that there was something wrong with Grandma.

———

There I was, hanging from the side of the mountain with Eric dangling below me. I knew that if I cut the line he would die, but if I didn't we would both die. I thought for a long moment and decided that I would try, with all of my might, to pull him up. I wasn't sure if I had enough strength left, but he was my friend and it was do or die. I took a deep breath and then, after quickly securing a verbal promise from him for a couple of hundred thousand dollars, I pulled him up to safety. Afterward, I knew Eric was grateful that I had saved his life, even if he was too proud to tell me.

———

And suddenly everything made sense. I knew what I had to do. I needed to quit my job. But before I could do that I needed to get a job to quit. Ideally, one that would suddenly make everything make sense when I quit it.

———

"Dad," we pleaded, "can we keep him?"
   He smiled and said, "Keep him? Hell, we're going to eat him."

———

I was talking to this guy at a party and he said, "'Can't' is not part of my vocabulary."
   I said, "Wow. You're not going to believe this, but something impossible just happened."
   "What's that?"
   "You just exceeded your vocabulary, at the beginning of that sentence you said there."
   Then someone got punched. I think it might have been me.

I used to have this poster on my bedroom wall that said, "I am me. I can do anything." Sometimes I would look at it and think, "Poster, you are in for a rude awakening."

———

I hadn't been home since the summer the synchronized swimming team drowned. It was tragic, but beautiful. Apparently, one of them got a cramp.

———

Someone was in the house. I was terrified. I stood still. I knew in these situations that the best thing to do was to get out of there. You're not supposed to try and fight. But at the same time, I really wanted to take the stereo. Plus, judging from the pictures of the home owner I saw on his desk, he seemed pretty small.

———

We started to see less and less of each other. And that's when I knew it was quicksand.

———

It was just after I turned twenty that my parents told me I was not adopted.

———

We used to take some of the smaller animals the taxidermist had stuffed and put them back into the woods. This would lead the other animals in the woods to think those animals had "attitudes." You'd see a forest squirrel go up to one of the stuffed ones and try to be friendly. The stuffed one would just stare off into space. Then to see the look on the other squirrel's face... it was great.

Years later, the taxidermist died. We found out he was buried. I always thought that was a wasted opportunity.

———

Winter became Spring and Spring became Summer. Then Summer became Fall and Fall turned to Autumn. By the time Autumn turned to Winter I realized that there had been a synonym in the seasons.

———

He shoved me. I shoved him back. The bar became silent.

"You got a problem?" he said, almost bursting out of his T-shirt.

"Do you want to step outside?" I replied.

"Let's go!" he said. He had a murderous look in his eye and a murderous earring in his ear, too.

A minute later we were outside. My veins were coursing with adrenaline. The crowd spilled out behind us, like some sort of jelly that likes to watch fights.

He held up his fists. "All right, you little—"

"Do you want to step more outside?" I asked. I pointed to the awning just above us. "We're not fully outside yet...because of the awning."

He looked up at the awning. "Um...Okay."

We moved over a little more, out from under the awning.

"Come on. Bring it on, little man," he said as he took a step towards me.

"Do you want to step over there?" I said.

He paused, and said, "We're outside now. What's the problem?"

"Oh, what are you, scared?" I replied.

"No. I'm not scared. Let's go over there."

We walked over there. The crowd followed.

"Now get ready to die," he said, stretching his enormous torso like a gorilla.

"No, I meant do you want to step over *there?*" I explained. I pointed. He looked.

"Just a little farther," I continued, still sounding pretty threatening. I knew this tactic wouldn't work for much longer, but by now we were pretty close to my car.

"All right. But that's it," he warned.

"Fine," I said.

We moved again. The crowd was ready for the fight. He looked at me. I looked at him and said, "What's that over there?" Then I ran for my car.

I can't tell you how much I wish I had left my car unlocked that night.

From what people tell me, I did manage to get to the car door for just a moment.

———

Camping with the family was a lot of fun, especially when we did it on purpose.

———

She was sexy. She had long hair and long legs. She had long arms, too. Her legs and hair were the parts that I found most attractive. Now that I think about it, her arms were really, really long. I don't remember her name, because everyone called her by her nickname, Ape Arms.

———

You never forget your first kiss. And that's what makes it so hard to forgive my uncle.

———

The Word Awards

The annual Word Awards were held last night at Vernacular Pavilion. Here are some of the ceremony's highlights.

The word *allege* was honored for being the all-time most overused word in television news. The winner allegedly beat the second-place word, *suspect*, by a wide margin. *Allege* denied allegations that it won only because reporters are allegedly too stupid to think of other words to use. *Allege* thanked all the reporters for their "insane repetition" of it, and confirmed allegations that it will continue to be overused by people who work in the news media, many of whom allegedly don't even know what *allege* means.

Whom received a Lifetime Achievement Award for its special service to pompous assholes. *Whom* extended a special thanks to people who "correct others who mistakenly use 'who,'" saying, "I dedicate this award to them, without whom this would have not been possible."

Sesquipedalian shared the award for Most Autological Word with *autological*. The winners beat out fellow nominees, *let-*

ters and *nominee* for the prize. *Winner* was, once again, barred from competition for being too presumptuous. *Presumptuous* was not available for comment but managed to irritate people nonetheless.

The Ensemble Award for the Least Frequently Used Combination of Words went to *I was wrong*, which was presented by last year's winner *I have a drinking problem*.

The word *word* was honored for officially regaining its intended meaning after spending more than two decades in hip-hop where it has meant "yes, that's correct." *Word* began its embarrassing stint there in the late twentieth century when young rappers paired it with *up* (e.g., "Are you going to come correct?" "*Word up.*") and soon thereafter started to appear without *up*. *Up*, meanwhile, had been recruited with *in* by the very same community, who used it to say things like "I was all *up in* there" for reasons that are still unclear.

The Award for the Word Used Most Frequently When It Is Not Actually Justified went to *awesome*, which narrowly beat out *genius*. Many were surprised that *literally* was not nominated, literally.

The Parlance Memorial Award, given to the word that is most frequently whispered, went to *cancer* again this year, continuing its remarkable streak.

Your and *you're* performed a short comedy routine about just how stupid people on social networking sites are. *Yore*, who is famously reclusive, delighted the assembled crowd with a surprise cameo during the routine.

The night's best-dressed word was *slanted*, who fittingly arrived on the red carpet in italics.

Albeit won the Award for the Word Least Likely to Appear in a Tattoo.

The Award for Best Comedy Word went to *cahoots*, beating out crowd favorite *fart* and longtime champion *titmouse*.

The ceremony was briefly interrupted by a loud group of *nucular* protesters, who demanded that *nucular* be recognized as a word. Spotted among the protesters were *idiot* and *supposebly* (who, like *nucular*, is not a word but is nonetheless uttered every day by many, many people in America).

The Vernacular Lifetime Achievement Award went to *invent* for coming up with itself.

Finally, the coveted Onomatopoeia Prize went to *shphlaah* for the sound of a fat man accidentally sitting on a calzone.

Goodbyes

I am bad at goodbyes. It's a problem I've had for as long as I can remember.

My parents once told me that even before I could talk I had trouble with goodbyes. As a baby, when someone said goodbye to me, I would stare back at them and loudly fill my diaper as I crawled onto their lap.

When I was a toddler my parents began to put me in the basement whenever it came time to say goodbye. If they didn't, when somebody said goodbye I would panic, do a little dance, and then run full-speed into the wall. I don't remember doing this. I was too young. But the permanent marks on the wall (and on my head) are pretty good evidence that this happened.

My mother and father tried to explain away my goodbye difficulties as a phase, but things only got worse when I entered elementary school. I became even more agitated during goodbyes, often yelling directly into people's faces and then breaking down in tears.

By the time I got to high school, I had developed a full-blown problem. If someone even uttered the word "goodbye" I would tackle them. I earned a reputation for being not only clingy but also "holdy" (because once I had the person on the ground I would hold them as hard as I could).

When I left for college I didn't know how to say goodbye to my family, so I just snuck out of the house the night before while everyone was sleeping. I think my parents understood that I needed to do that, even if they were a little hurt by it. Unfortunately, I somehow managed to ruin that goodbye after I ran into our dog, Buster, on my way out of the house. Saying goodbye to Buster proved to be so difficult that I ended up throwing him directly at my parents, who were sleeping.

It's strange that I am so bad at goodbyes. I mean, no one else in my family has a problem with them. I have an aunt who has trouble with "see you soons," but that's about it. What's even stranger is that I've always been very good at hellos.

If I'm meeting someone for the first time I can simply say "Hello." No problem. And I can also change it up pretty easily if the situation calls for it. For example, if I'm meeting an attractive woman for the first time I'll say, "Helll...llloo" in a very seductive way as I look her body up and down and slowly walk around her. Incidentally, in my experience it's amazing how many women are bad at hellos, often turning a hello immediately into a goodbye right after a man has skillfully greeted and circled them. But I guess that's no surprise when you consider how stuck-up a lot of women are.

Anyway, I thought that waving might be a good way to get better at goodbyes, so I focused on that for a while. But even waving presented challenges. Sure I can easily wave hello (I mean who can't?) but when I try to wave later on in the conversation, as a goodbye, I get tripped up and just end up saying "hello" again.

Sometimes, to avoid the inevitable awkwardness, instead of saying goodbye I'll just keep the conversation going. Then I don't have to deal with the goodbye at all. That's not always the best tactic, though. I once ended up getting married because of it. When the relationship finally did end, the best I could do was "toodles." Man, that definitely did not help things when our divorce went to trial.

I saw a therapist for a while. Whenever I went to see him we would stand in his office and say goodbye to each other for the entire session, which inevitably put a lot of pressure on the end of every session. It often made leaving his office very confusing. Part of the problem, he told me, is that I suffer from what is called "separation anxiety" coupled with a more serious condition called "separation aggression."

While therapy didn't cure me, it did help. I got pretty good at saying other things instead of "goodbye," like "I'm going over there now" or "I am not going to stay here anymore." I learned that if I make an announcement about the next thing I'm going to do, that works quite well (i.e., "I am now going to get into this taxi" or "I'm going to go into that bathroom now and take a dump").

Part of the problem is that I just can't read situations that well. If we're saying goodbye to each other, I don't know if we should hug or kiss on the cheek, or just hold legs. I end up guessing. So far I've been wrong every time that I've guessed "hold legs."

My friend John is so good at goodbyes. He can say anything and it sounds right, like "Cheerio" or "Peace" or "I'll see you in Hell." That guy is prolific at goodbyes. Not me. I probably couldn't even say goodbye to someone who was falling off a cliff. The best I could do is shrug and make a face like, "Well, what can you do about cliffs?"

It's not all bad though. When I want to seem distant, not being able to say goodbye works well for me. One time I broke up with this girl and she said, "Goodbye." I didn't say anything. Then she said, "Aren't you going to say anything?" I said, "No U-turns." She walked away, thinking that I said something deep. But I was just reading a nearby sign out loud.

People sometimes ask me what I'm going to say when it comes time to die. I honestly don't know. I'll probably go "Ughhh" and make believe that I died. And then, after everyone leaves, I'll really die. But I bet by then our society will have robots that can help you say goodbye, or there will be some sort of self-puppeting thing you can hook up to yourself to do it for you.

Hey, look! What's that behind you?

The End.